James Thompson

An Essay on English Municipal History

James Thompson

An Essay on English Municipal History

ISBN/EAN: 9783741163272

Manufactured in Europe, USA, Canada, Australia, Japa

Cover: Foto ©ninafisch / pixelio.de

Manufactured and distributed by brebook publishing software (www.brebook.com)

James Thompson

An Essay on English Municipal History

AN ESSAY

ON

ENGLISH

MUNICIPAL HISTORY.

BY

JAMES THOMPSON,

AUTHOR OF A HISTORY OF LEICESTER FROM THE TIME OF THE ROMANS
TO THE END OF THE SEVENTEENTH CENTURY.

LONDON:
LONGMANS, GREEN, AND CO.
1867.

LEICESTER:
WARD AND SONS, PRINTERS, WELLINGTON STREET.

TO

THOMAS TERTIUS PAGET, Esq.,

OF HUMBERSTONE,

THE HEREDITARY FRIEND OF MUNICIPAL FREEDOM,

AND FIRM SUPPORTER OF CIVIL AND RELIGIOUS LIBERTY,

THIS VOLUME IS DEDICATED,

AS A MARK OF ESTEEM AND RESPECT,

BY THE AUTHOR.

CONTENTS.

	PAGE
INTRODUCTION	vii

CHAPTER I.
THE ROMAN-BRITISH MUNICIPALITIES 1

CHAPTER II.
SAXON TOWN INSTITUTIONS 8

CHAPTER III.
THE BOROUGH OF ST. ALBANS 16

CHAPTER IV.
THE BOROUGH OF LEICESTER 32

CHAPTER V.
BOROUGH OF LEICESTER (*Continued*) 49

CHAPTER VI.
BOROUGH OF LEICESTER (*Continued*) 65

CHAPTER VII.
BOROUGH OF LEICESTER (*Concluded*) 80

CHAPTER VIII.
THE BOROUGH OF PRESTON 91

CHAPTER IX.
THE CITY OF NORWICH 110

CHAPTER X.
THE CITY OF NORWICH (*Continued*) 123

CHAPTER XI.
THE CITY OF NORWICH (*Concluded*) 129

CHAPTER XII.
THE BOROUGH OF YARMOUTH 137

CHAPTER XIII.
ON MARKET TOWNS NOT INCORPORATED 146

CHAPTER XIV.
ON MARKET TOWNS NOT INCORPORATED (*Concluded*) . . 163

CHAPTER XV.
MUNICIPAL INSIGNIA 173

CHAPTER XVI.
THE FRENCH COMMUNES 180

CHAPTER XVII.
A COMPARISON BETWEEN THE FRENCH COMMUNES AND ENGLISH BOROUGHS 186

CHAPTER XVIII.
PRACTICAL CONCLUSIONS 193

"It would indeed be but slight philosophy to suppose that any one set of circumstances would account for the infinite variety which the history of towns presents. Though there are features of resemblance common to them all, yet each has its peculiar story, its peculiar conditions of progress and decay; even as the children of one family, which bear a likeness to each other, yet have each its own tale of joy and sorrow, of smiles and tears, of triumph and failure."—KEMBLE's *Saxons in England*, v. 2, p. 307.

INTRODUCTION.

The state of the ancient boroughs of this island, in regard to their local government, has furnished a fruitful theme to political enquirers during the two last centuries. Theories have been advanced and conjectures hazarded on this subject of the most varied nature. While some writers have ascribed the origin of English municipalities to the institutions introduced by the Romans, others have referred them to the Saxon population. While, on the one hand, the attempt has been made to prove that we owe all our local liberties to the monarchs of the country flourishing subsequent to the Norman Conquest, on the other, arguments have been employed to establish that those liberties were enjoyed before the monarchs in question existed. While, again, by some jurists, the old Corporations of England have been identified with the more ancient manorial Courts, by another authority their origin has been found in the Merchant Guilds of primitive times.

Perhaps the earliest formal treatise upon the subject is that of Dr. Brady,* who maintains that the ancient boroughs of this country derived their existence from the "bounty" of the Anglo-Norman monarchs, and that they were developed, in some instances at least, from the Merchant Guilds. But when it is added that this author wrote in

* *An Historical Treatise of English Boroughs.*

the reign of James the Second, and that his purpose was, it would seem, to justify the arbitrary proceedings of that king, in taking away the charters from the incorporated towns, on seeking to establish an autocratic authority, suspicion falls upon his theory; though he may not be in all respects wrong in his conclusions—as, for example, in those relating to the Merchant Guilds.

Far more important than Dr. Brady's History of the Boroughs, however, in the range of its enquiries—far more complete in its plan and legitimate in its purpose—was the "History of Boroughs and Municipal Corporations" by Sergeant Merewether and Mr. Archibald John Stephens, barrister-at-law, whose work (published in 1835) is a monument of extensive research and profound erudition. — Its purpose was to prove that while boroughs were in existence, in the Saxon period and subsequently—by the term "borough" meaning a town having a jurisdiction separate from that of the surrounding rural districts— municipal "corporations" were unknown until the commencement of the reign of Henry VI., when a charter of incorporation was granted to the inhabitants of Kingston-upon-Hull; and that it was not until more than a century later that boroughs generally became known as "Corporations."

The attention of the present writer was drawn to the subject of this Essay while collecting the materials of a local history and investigating the origin of a Corporation. Among the mass of ancient documents to which access was allowed him, were numerous parchment rolls of great length, purporting to be those of a Merchant Guild. In order to ascertain what this body was, the writer had recourse for information to the authorities already named; but he found that neither in the work of Brady nor in that of Merewether and Stephens did he meet with a solution of his difficulties, and therefore he returned to the archives themselves, resolving to study their contents more closely than ever, and to extract from them every ray of light they would afford in illustration of the subject of his enquiry. The results are epitomized in the fourth, fifth, and sixth chapters of this Essay, which the writer believes place the question in a true, novel, and interesting position; because they embody facts derived from the records of our ancestors themselves, who thus speak to us in a manner directly, as if long centuries had not intervened since the characters were inscribed by their own hands on the now mouldering vellum.

Briefly stated, these are the conclusions at which the writer arrived:

That before the Incorporation of the borough whose history he was enquiring into took place, its inhabitants generally were members of a Merchant Guild; that at their head was the Mayor of the Guild; that a Council of the Guild was periodically chosen; that they admitted new members every year, to whom an oath of allegiance to the Guild was administered; that they kept a yearly account of receipts and expenses; that they levied local taxation; that they repaired the gates, walls, and bridges of the town; that they had frequent public meals of bread and wine at the common expense; that they were known as the "Community of the Guild"; that from none but their own body were their officers chosen; and that, in fact, the whole area of municipal administration was occupied by the Guild Merchant, which was the governing body of the town in regard to all matters except the enforcement of the civil and criminal law—the latter devolving on the ".Portmanmote," an institution identical in its nature and jurisdiction with the Court Leet of the borough. The writer further concluded that the Merchant Guild merged in the Corporation erected in the reign of Queen Elizabeth, and that the members of the Guild acquired the name of "freemen" at the same period.*

In order to avoid misapprehension, it may be well to explain that there is a general sense and a legal sense in which the word "Corporation" is employed. In the former, the ruling body in a borough has often been so designated; but in the latter, the term is strictly confined to communities to whom a royal charter has been conceded, empowering them to hold estates in succession, to sell property, to sue and be sued under a common name, and to exercise other functions. By historical writers the word has been freely used in the general sense, and to signify the conferring of independent and separate jurisdiction upon the people of a particular locality; but before the fifteenth and sixteenth centuries, the word was wholly unknown in its application to boroughs, and it was only after the reign of Queen Elizabeth that town 'Corporations (the word being an abbreviation of "Incorporation") were recognized among the institutions of the country. Anterior to that date, the governing body in every leading medieval borough was called "the Guild," and even to this day a vestige of the institution is left in the name of the usual place of meeting of the town councils, which is still often called the Guild Hall, that is, the Hall of the Guild.

It may be well here to observe that in the Middle Ages various institutions called "Guilds" were established, having different objects to promote, with which the Merchant Guild should not be for a moment confounded. Ecclesiastical and

---

* Some of the results of the writer's enquiries have been published in detached portions: in the first instance, in a paper read at the Congress of the British Archæological Association at Winchester, in 1845; and subsequently in the *Gentleman's Magazine*, in 1851, in three papers entitled "the Municipal Franchises of the Middle Ages, illustrated by documents from the Archives of Leicester."

INTRODUCTION.   xi

Trade Guilds, for example, were in operation contemporaneously with the Merchant Guilds; but while the former of the two strictly confined themselves to the payment of mass-priests, employed to say prayers in the hope of releasing the souls of deceased members from purgatory, the latter were intended to be composed exclusively of masters and workmen, whose object was to regulate the affairs of those who were engaged in one particular department of commerce and industry; and therefore such societies were entirely distinct from the Merchant Guild, which comprised persons connected with all trades, in a union intended for common municipal purposes.

It might appear to some readers that the institution here described existed exceptionally in Leicester, and therefore that the details presented in the following pages respecting it have no interest beyond the locality; but it is believed by the writer that the deeper and wider the enquiry made in municipal archives, the more fully will the truth appear, that in every borough of ancient origin, a reference to the charters will prove the presence of the Merchant Guild, as the sole municipal body known to the inhabitants, before the Incorporation of such borough. If so, the internal regulations will be found in the main identical with those explained as in operation at Leicester in former periods, which thus acquire unusual interest; since no details of a similar nature have ever before been published in any work on municipal institutions.

At the same time, while insisting on the fact of the early establishment of the Merchant Guilds in the old English boroughs, it will be perceived by the reader of the following chapters that town-communities, in possession of local liberties and privileges, were formerly to be met with in various stages of progress, capable of division into two principal classes: 1. Towns in which Court Leets exercised a jurisdiction, and the inhabitants elected their own bailiff, but which were only quasi-boroughs, as the Sheriff of the county occasionally exercised power within their limits. 2. Towns in which Merchant Guilds were in action, and which enjoyed full town-rights, having their Aldermen or Mayors, and their Councils. Of the class named first, Manchester, St. Albans, and perhaps the market-towns unincorporated (see chapter thirteen), were examples; of the second class, Leicester, Preston, Yarmouth, and perhaps Norwich, (see the fourth, fifth, sixth, seventh, and following chapters) furnish instances.

It is to assist all readers who take an interest in the rise of our Municipal Freedom, in their enquiries into the subject; and to serve as a contribution to the English literature relating to it; that the author has compiled this brief Essay.

Leicester, April 13, 1867.

ON ENGLISH MUNICIPAL HISTORY.

CHAPTER I.

THE ROMAN BRITISH MUNICIPALITIES.

BEFORE the close of the Roman Dominion in this Island, many large cities were standing in its numerous districts. Most of these were surrounded by walls of great height and thickness, to which towers, placed at intervals, gave an aspect of majestic and imposing strength. At the massive gateways sentinels were daily posted to guard against the entrance of unwelcome and hostile intruders. Within the walls were edifices, public and private, of a stateliness worthy the exterior of these cities. Courthouses surrounded by lofty colonnades; spacious marketplaces surrounded by well-built houses; baths handsome without and commodious within; temples with porticoes whose pediments were supported by classic columns—were then as familiar to the eyes of the residents as the town-halls, market-houses, churches, chapels, and theatres of our modern towns are to their inhabitants. Among the private dwellings were many on which had been lavished rich and rare adornment, and wherein every possible arrangement had been made to minister to the luxurious enjoyment of their owners. Tesselated pavements of elaborate device covered the floors, designs of beauty decorated the walls, furniture convenient and useful filled the rooms, hypocausts warmed and lamps lighted the interiors, and baths were found in recesses of the buildings. Near these towns also were amphitheatres, where bands of itinerant gladiators and proprietors of wild beasts periodically furnished sanguinary shows to the populace.

The inhabitants were of an origin very mixed and indefinitely composite. Undoubtedly among the higher classes, who were principally the rulers, were many persons in whose veins flowed pure Italian blood; and there was probably a considerable proportion who were descendants of the ancient British race; but largely intermingled with these were the progeny of the auxiliary soldiers of Rome—recruits from every part of ancient Europe—from countries known to us in the present day as Greece, Germany, France, Spain, Portugal, Belgium—and even from the Northern Coast of Africa. Still, whatever might have been their race, all had learnt to speak Latin, and they obeyed the Roman laws and were governed by Roman institutions.

Unfortunately for the historian, very little positive information is to be obtained concerning the municipal arrangements of the country at this period. We learn from Tacitus that in the latter half of the first century towns were rapidly springing up, and most probably on the sites of the encampments formed during the wars in which the natives were subjugated. The Roman author also describes the aptitude with which the Britons adapted themselves to the institutions, the manners, and the costume of the conquerors. In the various places, institutions suitable to the purposes of the latter were established, when the work of pacification was completed. Where the Romans themselves were from the first present in large numbers, we may suppose, the municipal organization more nearly resembled that of the parent city, than in those towns where the British, or people of another race, formed the majority of the population; and there were intermediate stages of either dependence or freedom, measured by the different circumstances of different communities. We are told[*] that the first rank among Roman-British cities was claimed by the

[*] The authority for the statements in the text is Richard of Cirencester, of whose genuineness modern critics are sceptical; but his observations correspond remarkably well with what might be conjectured to be the state of affairs in the island at the time to which he refers.

COLONIES, each of which was on a small scale a representation of the city of Rome; adopting the same customs, being governed by the same laws, and being ruled by magistrates on whom similar titles conferred a similar authority. The inhabitants of the Colonies are supposed to have been Roman veterans, who had been rewarded with a portion of the lands of the conquered natives, and they were settled in situations combining the double advantage of a fruitful soil and a military position. Their sons also were obliged to be enrolled in the army as soon as they attained the years of manhood. Of these Colonies, it is said, there were nine in Britain—two of a civil, seven of a military description. These were Bath, Caerleon, Chester, Chesterfield, Colchester, Gloucester, Lincoln, London, and Richborough; and, as the enumeration indicates, they were well distributed for military purposes throughout South Britain.

Other towns occupied a secondary rank, possessing, however, privileges in some respects superior to those enjoyed by the Colonies: these were the MUNICIPIA, in which the inhabitants were exempted from the operation of the imperial statutes, and, with the proud title of Roman citizens, exercised the right of choosing their own magistrates and of enacting their own laws. York and St. Alban's were the only municipal cities in Britain before the reign of Antoninus [138 A. D.]

A third class of towns were endowed with the LATIAN RIGHT. In these, the inhabitants chose their own magistrates, who, at the expiration of their year of office, claimed the freedom of Rome—an object of ambition to provincial residents, which was secured by the expedient of annual elections, and was thus successively conferred on almost all the members of each Latin Corporation. The number of these places was ten: Blackrode, Caister (Lincolnshire), Carlisle, Catterick, Cirencester, Dunbarton, Inverness, Perth, Salisbury, and Slack in Longwood.

Lowest in rank were the STIPENDIARY TOWNS, which were compelled to pay tribute, and were governed by Roman officers, who received their appointment from the pretor of the province. In this class were Caer Segont, Caerwent, Caermarthen, Canterbury, Caistor near Norwich, Dorchester, Exeter, Leicester, High Rochester, Rochester (Kent), Vindonum (Hampshire), and Winchester.* It seems not improbable that the dependency of these places on the Roman authorities was attributable to the fact of their being populated mainly by natives, or auxiliary soldiers and settlers of foreign descent; their preponderance requiring the maintenance over them of an exclusively imperial authority.

Although at some one time, perhaps, the whole of the Roman stations might be classified as just described, yet it may be inferred that the less privileged were always striving to be placed on a footing of equality with the more privileged places. The obtainment of the freedom of the city being associated with a participation in the benefit of the Roman laws, particularly in reference to marriage, testaments, and inheritances, every provincial of any rank or opulence was ambitious to possess the *status* thereby conferred. In this way, the Municipal Cities gradually rose to the position of the Colonies, and the Latian and Stipendiary Towns followed in the same direction. In the reigns of the Antonines [138 to 180 A.D.] the freedom of the city was bestowed on the greater proportion of their subjects, and Caracalla [211 to 217 A.D.] extended it to the whole body of the natives; his object being thus to raise a larger amount of taxation by increasing the numbers of those on whom it could be imposed.

Subsequent to the reign of Caracalla, therefore, all the towns enjoyed the rights of Roman citizens. Those which

* The foregoing classification has been adopted from Lingard's *History*

have already been designated, consisted not merely of the places themselves surrounded by their walls, but of a certain extent of land around them. They had a government of their own, resembling that of the ancient constitution of Rome, and exempt from all control of the imperial officers. As soldiers, the inhabitants were obliged to defend only their own town, and were not liable to serve elsewhere. Speaking generally, the Roman *municipium*, or town corporation, consisted of the people at large and the governing body. The people were known as the *plebs*—the governing body as the *curia*. The *plebs* elected an important officer called *defensor civitatis*—the defender of the city—their advocate and champion in cases of oppression by the *curia*, or senate. The members of the governing body were designated *curiales* or *decuriones*. They enjoyed their rank by hereditary right; they received various emoluments and enjoyed special and important privileges; and they elected the magistrates of the city. The two chief magistrates were named *duumviri*, and were usually elected yearly; in addition to whom were the *principales*, chosen to serve for fifteen years, and who were the administrators of the municipal affairs, and formed the permanent council of the governing body. Besides these, there were various inferior officers, also elected by the *curia*.*

History furnishes us with little, if any, insight into the state of the municipalities of Roman Britain, and the discoveries of archæologists add but scantily to the light thus supplied. We learn that on an altar found at Elenborough (Olenacum) in Cumberland, it is recorded that Gaius Cornelius Peregrinus, Tribune of the Cohort, from the Province of Mauritania Cæsariensis, built or restored the houses and chapel *(domos et ædem)* of the Decurions.

* *The Celt, the Roman, and the Saxon,* by Thomas Wright, Esq., p. 360, 1st edition.

In another inscription, mention is made of a Decurion of the colony of Gloucester, who died at Bath. In larger communities the name of Senator was given to the Decurions; a Flavius Martius being thus spoken of in an inscription found at Penrith.—Another class of civic officers, designated Sevirs, was commemorated on an inscription found upon a sarcophagus at York; a Roman citizen, named Marcus Verecundus Diogenes, having been styled a "Sevir of the colony of York." These functionaries appear, however, to have been identical with the Augustales —members of a priestly corporation instituted in honor of the Augustan family, who received the dignity under a decree of the Decurious, and were not entrusted with any municipal authority.*—In addition to these officers, inscriptions at Castle Carey in Scotland, at Chichester, and at Bath mention certain institutions called *collegia*, which seem to correspond to the trade companies of a later period. That at Chichester refers to a *collegium fabrorum*; that at Bath to a *collegium fabricensium*†—a smith's company.

The position of the Decurions, who constituted the Town Councils of the Roman period, was, at least in the reigns of Constantine and his successors, onerous and undesirable; for on them were imposed the laborious offices which could be productive only of envy and reproach, and by the imperial authority they were condemned to bear the burdens of civil society,‡ and to be responsible for all deficiencies. Deprived of the power of selling their landed property without permission of the governor of the city, in order to prevent its passing to an owner less capable of paying

* See paper " On the Sarcophagus of Marcus Verecundus Diogenes and the Civil Administration of Roman York," by the Rev. John Kenrick, M.A.; also, "Eburacum," by the Rev. C. Wellbeloved.

† *The Celt, the Roman, and the Saxon*, page 361, first edition.

‡ Gibbon's *Decline and Fall of the Roman Empire*, chapter 17.

taxes; limited in the disposal of their property, if childless, by being able to bequeath only a third part of it—the rest devolving to the Curia; and prevented from leaving their places of residence, even for a short period, without the prefect's authority,—the Decurions were in a condition which in the present day would be regarded as intolerable. In return for all that they had to endure, they were permitted to solace themselves with the empty honour of possessing the title of the *splendidissimus ordo*—the "most splendid order."

After the reign of Caracalla, when (as we have seen) the freedom of the city was given to all the inhabitants of the Roman British stations alike, this island therefore contained a large number of communities, which, after payment of taxes to the imperial authority, were left free to govern themselves, independently of all external interference in their municipal affairs. If the statements of Richard of Cirencester be correct, there would be not fewer than thirty-three—while the names in the survey of Ptolemy, supposed to have been compiled about A.D. 320, show fifty-six—of these miniature Republics, existing in Britain in the four hundred years elapsing between the reigns of Claudius and Theodorus the younger.

Of none of these have any written records survived, and concerning the impression they left on succeeding ages we are left to conjecture and to speculate. But our view of English Municipal History would have been imperfect, had we not brought under notice the fragments of knowledge here presented.

CHAPTER II.

SAXON TOWN INSTITUTIONS.

On the departure of the Romans, the bond uniting the British Towns was removed; they were no longer confederated under one supreme head, and capable of presenting a phalanx of resistance, if need was, to an enemy; they became so many separate and detached bodies, each acting by itself and for itself, and perhaps in some cases rivalries and enmities existed among them, and armed collisions had taken place between their inhabitants. Alliances and counter-alliances might also have been formed between others of the municipalities. To these causes of disunion may be added the fact, which is now clearly established, that in certain stations the people being almost wholly of one race—perhaps Teutonic, perhaps Gaulish, though more often the former—invited from Germany and France immigrants to settle among them, and thus antagonisms of race as well as of interest and policy supervened. It is stated, on the authority of inscriptions and other monuments,* that the population of the towns was becoming more and more Teutonic by the arrival of recruits from the Continent, as the close of the Roman rule drew near; until, at length, "there can be little doubt that German blood predominated, to a great extent, in many of the Roman cities in Britain."

When this disintegration of the political system of the island was completed, the progress of invasion must have been rapid. As tribe after tribe of Saxons and Angles pressed inland, the cities became a prey, more or less easy, to the fierce and irresistible invaders; in those places where their kinsmen were settled, they were admitted

---

* *The Celt, the Roman, and the Saxon,* c 13.

within the walls by consent, and probably under compact—in other cases, they besieged the terrified and comparatively powerless townsmen, and overwhelmed them by their ferocity and their numbers.

Here two questions arise :—

1st. Did the Saxons ultimately become the inhabitants of the Roman-British towns? and

2nd. Did they introduce into them, for purposes of government, their own local institutions?

It must be taken as a fact, that the Romanized population of the British cities habitually employed the Latin language down to the latest period of the existence of the Roman authority in this island, and that they would have continued to do so, had no influence interfered to prevent them. This is obvious; as the unlearning of one language, and the adoption of another, is one of the most difficult proceedings to which any people can be induced to submit. In the case of a complete conquest, or the expulsion of the inhabitants of a district from their abodes, the change is, however, probable. Now, we know that the Latin tongue ceased to be spoken in the British towns, the Saxon being substituted for it; and that the towns themselves received new names from the invaders: the inference would be, therefore, that the general introduction of the Saxon language followed the possession of the towns by the Saxons.

If the towns became occupied by the people of that race, and the ancient language was also superseded by the use of their own, then we may infer the probability that, in all such cases, the institutions of the conquerors supplanted those of the former inhabitants.

If we turn our attention to another country, where the Roman influences were not destroyed—where no conquest, corresponding at least in extent and effect to that of Britain by the Saxons, was accomplished—then we shall find a state of things there prevailing exactly as it might have been predicated from the pre-existing circumstances. In France, the Roman conquest was universal in its influence; most of the towns, especially those in the South, remained under the Roman officials through the centuries in which, in this country, the Saxons were establishing their institutions and using their language daily in their habitations and the districts they occupied. In France, then, the Roman municipal system persisted in maintaining itself; the Latin language was not disused, but formed the basis of modern French; the names of many of the ancient cities are simply corruptions of the Latin names—not new designations; and the titles of the municipal functionaries are derived direct from those recognized in the Roman period. But, it can scarcely be doubted, had a Romanized population retained the ownership of the Roman British cities, and preserved their municipal regulations, the language would have remained in great part Latinized, the towns would have been known by their Latinized names, and the town officers would have been known to this day by Latin titles; while it is historically authenticated, that within a few centuries after the departure of the Romans the Saxon tongue had become the vernacular, the towns were known by Saxon names, and the designations of officials were given in the language of the people. To show the difference in this latter respect, it may be mentioned that while in France the Latin terms "prefect" and "consul" were adhered to as the names of the chief officers of the municipalities, in England the Saxon words "alderman" and "portreeve" were used instead; the designation "mayor" having been introduced, subsequent to the Norman conquest, from the Continent. It may be inferred, then, that the Saxons, with their language, brought their forms of local government into operation in this country, in the period intervening between the withdrawal of the Roman garrisons, and the date when the Roman names of towns disappeared and they gave way to those by which they are at present known, with slight modifications.

We have to assume that when the invasion by the Saxons had proved generally successful, and the land had fallen into the hands of its new owners, the chief of these constituted, in their own domains, the rulers—or, to select a term in modern use, the "lords of the manors." To them, by a nominal delegation from the sovereign, was imparted authority over all their tenants and the residents upon their estates. They held their courts, in which all males were obliged to be enrolled at a certain age, to find two friends to be securities for them, and to appear at stated periods yearly. In these courts (called Courts Leet) the steward or deputy of the manorial lord presided, and justice was done—the criminal laws being therein administered, and civil suits being therein determined. The jurisdiction was necessarily limited and defined—other courts, as those of the County and the Hundred, having greater authority, and being appealed to in cases where the manorial courts were supposed to be incompetent to the final arbitrement of weighty matters of controversy.

In the rural districts this system had, perhaps, its original and primitive seat, and was brought into this country from Germany by the invaders, who had been accustomed to it in the scattered communities of their fatherland; but it was capable of adaptation to the requirements of townsmen. We may ascertain what the system had become shortly before the Norman Conquest, by referring to the Laws of Edward the Confessor, in which the various powers of the lords of the manors are minutely detailed. In the twenty-second of those laws they are stated to be Soc, Sac, Theam, and Infangtheof. Under these obsolete terms are disguised the right to have jurisdiction over a domain, in settling various pleas and suits that might arise among tenants, and the power of punishing theft (Soc); the right to take the fines or forfeits imposed at the courts (Sac); the right of persons living in the manor to buy and sell (Theam); and the right to punish a thief belonging to another district, if he robbed a tenant and were captured in the lordship (Infangtheof). To these were added, usually, Outfangtheof—the right to follow and punish a thief who fled to another district* than that to which he belonged; and Toll—the right to levy local taxes.

It will be perceived that here are the rude germs of local self-government. When towns became populous, and communities acquired sufficient unity of purpose and character, they sought to procure from the monarch, or the lord of the manor, either by agreement or purchase, the same authority as that he himself possessed. In such an event, the townsmen in their communal character became entitled to appoint their own steward or bailiff to preside in the Court Leet, and to decide pleas and to punish offenders—selected a jury or juries among themselves—and put into a common purse the fees levied upon the suitors in the courts and the fines imposed upon convicted criminals. It is not improbable the lord of the manor would find it ultimately advantageous to transfer his powers absolutely, or for a term of years, to the townsmen, on consideration of receiving, without the trouble of collection, as large a sum annually as he had previously derived from his own bailiff, with whom he had to share the receipts. Beginning in this way, by compounding with their lord for the exercise of his prerogative, it is only in the course of events to

---

* *Infangtheof* and *Outfangtheof* may really be rendered "In-caught-thief" and "Out-caught-thief."

suppose the townsmen would eventually procure a still greater extension of the principle of self-government, and would acquire greater ability for its exercise.

It will have been perceived that the Court Leet had relation more especially to criminal administration and civil suits or pleas, than to strictly municipal affairs. Another institution came into existence, therefore, the purpose of which was the settlement of the latter, and which in due time rose to high importance—we mean the Merchants' Guild. Its constitution, at the early date to which allusion is here made, it is difficult to ascertain. But it seems highly probable that the home of the Guild System was Germany. It originated in the sacrificial feasts of the Heathen times,* and was modified on the introduction of Christianity. Even before towns were formed there, to any great extent, sworn brotherhoods had arisen, whose members were closely bound to each other as the members of one family; but when the towns had grown up into existence, these brotherhoods were most readily constituted, and they succeeded in gradually freeing themselves from the burdens connected with their place of residence, or to which the inhabitants were subjected by powerful authority. By degrees they acquired for themselves privileges from the chief ruler of the country, or from the authority to which the place belonged, and to whom the royal dues were paid in greater or less amount. "Guild" and "Town Community" were then conceptions of the same significance; and guild-right was in many instances synonymous with town-right.†

In England, in most of the ancient boroughs, Merchant Guilds were established in the Saxon period. It is related that Ethelwulph, king of the West Saxons (*circa* 850 A.D.)

---

* See Dr. Wilda's *Das Gildenwesen im Mittelalter*. Leipsic, 1831.

† *Das Gildenwesen im Mittelalter*, section 4.

granted to the inhabitants of Winchester the privilege of forming such a society*; and as the progress of towns was generally simultaneous, we may infer the institution of similar guilds, or clubs, in other places of importance was nearly contemporaneous, if not earlier in date. The order of their development may be thus supposed: When, in the Roman-British towns, the state of security to person and property had become more or less complete, after the conquest by the Saxons (which, it may be presumed, was not until the middle or close of the seventh century), and the inhabitants occupied in trade began, however moderately, to acquire wealth, a class of this kind was formed in every place. The term "merchant" is probably the translation from the medieval Latin of the word "mercator," which was deemed the equivalent of the old Saxon word "chapman," and this designated the townsmen who were tradesmen. They were, however, a class different from what is now in existence in the same position. They were persons who either wove rude cloth at the loom, or collected the raw materials of manufacture (wool, for example), or articles of daily consumption, and conveyed them to fairs and markets in towns adjacent, on their shoulders or on pack-horses; for the traffic of the places in which they lived was manifestly inadequate to their maintenance. Each owned or occupied a small plot of ground (a "burgage") on which his dwelling was erected. They were not only liable to the taxes imposed on them by the kings, or thanes, or abbots, on or near whose domains they dwelt, but they were exposed to numerous exactions on their way to other towns, and in these towns, too, on their arrival. They were also placed in peril, and subject to obstructions, whenever they journeyed to distant localities. These incidents of difficulty and danger gave them, therefore, a common interest in their

* Dr. Milner's *History of Winchester*.

mutual safety and mutual exemption from legalized pillage. In such circumstances, doubtless, the Merchants' or Chapmens' Guilds had their origin. Their members were bound to each other by oaths and pledges, and they paid a common contribution to the purse of the brotherhood. They built by their united funds a Guild Hall, wherein they met to transact their affairs, and occasionally to feast together. They punished fraud, committed by one guild brother upon another. They assisted each other in times of sickness and adversity. They clubbed together to purchase charters of freedom from kings and lords, to repair the town walls, and to promote other public objects. Being composed of free men, and including all the more energetic, thriving, and able inhabitants, the Merchants' Guilds became by successive steps, what were subsequently called the Corporations of Boroughs. It was by them, in all probability, a transfer of the powers of the Court Leet from the lords of manors to the townspeople was effected by purchase; and as independence of jurisdiction, and self-government in local affairs, virtually constituted a Borough, they were the persons who were styled, in charters and public documents, " burgesses" and " good men of the town."

In the Chapters which follow, the author has attempted to illustrate, in separate histories, and in actual operation, the principles already explained. With this view he has selected the example of St. Alban's—a place where the Roman influence wholly ceased to exist; of Leicester, once the seat of the Roman authority, and where the ancient archives so forcibly confirm what has been said concerning the Guild Merchant; of Preston, a town of Saxon origin, still preserving its Custumale, which throws so much light on the internal administration of an early medieval borough; and other instances.

CHAPTER III.

THE BOROUGH OF ST. ALBAN'S.

In that long era which elapsed between the reigns of Claudius and the ephemeral emperors who immediately succeeded Honorius, in the fifth century, the place known to the Romans by the name VERULAMIUM was existing near the site of the modern St. Alban's. It then shared, with London and Colchester, the reputation of being one of the most populous and prosperous of British cities. In evidence of its populousness, it may be stated that Tacitus records, that in an insurrection of the natives, as many as 70,000 Roman citizens and their allies, resident in these three towns, were slaughtered by the insurgents. At this time it had acquired the importance of a *Municipium*—a place in which all the inhabitants enjoyed the privilege only conceded in other towns to Roman soldiers and citizens. In the course of time it became so large, as that its boundaries included an area estimated to have been one hundred acres in extent. To the north, a lake covering twenty acres—on the southern, eastern, and western sides a strong wall and deep ditch—formed its defences. Within these limits stood the dwellings of a civilized community, composed of the governor of the station, the magistrates, the council, the soldiers, the priests, the rich traders, and the humble artizans; with the court-house, the forum, the temples, the baths, and other public structures. We may infer its *status* as a city from the fact that its name is inscribed on coins of the empire, being probably once familiar to the inhabitants of the great city itself.

In the latter half of the third century there was living in Verulamium a person named Albanus, who was a native of the place. He had been to Rome, where he served for seven years as a soldier under the Emperor Dioclesian.

While in the imperial city, it is not improbable he had imbibed the doctrines of Christianity from some of the numerous disciples then living within its walls; or, if he had not actually been converted, he had received impressions favourable to those doctrines; for we learn from the ecclesiastical writers,* that he entertained in his house in Verulamium, a certain priest of Christ, who fled from his persecutors, when the cruel proceedings initiated by Dioclesian's order, against the Christians in Italy, were carried out in the cities of Britain. Albanus, or Alban, secretly sheltered the priest in his house for some time; and while he watched the good man pray, day after day, he insensibly became fully convinced in his own mind of the truth of the religion of Christ. But the circumstance of the concealment of the priest by Albanus became known to the Roman governor of the city, who sent soldiers to take him into custody. When, however, Alban saw them, he offered himself, instead of his guest, in the garment which the latter customarily wore. On being taken before the governor, his assumption of the priest's habit was immediately detected; and his voluntary surrender of himself in place of the priest so much enraged the governor, that he ordered Alban to endure whatever torments were due to the priest, if he persisted in the "new superstition" (as Christianity was then designated). Alban was immediately called upon to offer sacrifice to the gods under pain of suffering death; and, refusing to do so, was subjected to horrible and novel torments, which he bore with astonishing patience and heroic fortitude. He was finally beheaded. A variety of fables are mixed up with the tradition of the Protomartyr of England; but, stripped of what is untrue and fabulous, this would seem to be the true story.

* *Bede's Ecclesiastical History*, the *Works of Gildas*, and *Butler's Lives of the Saints*.

When the Romans abandoned this island, the city of Verulamium fell rapidly into decay. The site was quite deserted, and the ruins of its once splendid edifices served only as places of concealment for thieves and robbers. But the legend of Alban always hovered over the spot, and his bones, having been collected and buried near to the city by those who venerated his memory, a sacred interest was always attached to the place in the estimation of true believers, and the martyr was canonized by the Church of Rome.

For more than four centuries the legend was cherished; and as it passed from one generation to another by oral tradition, it doubtless received the addition of particulars of miracles which rendered it increasingly acceptable in an age of credulity and ignorance. At last it became fixed, with all its marvellous details, in the history of Bede, the monk of Yarmouth, whose work was made known to the world in manuscript in the year 731. It seems probable that this history was read in the households of the Anglo-Saxon kings, and that among those who were acquainted with its contents was Offa, the king of the Mercians, who obtained his throne in the year 755. He was a cruel and rapacious ruler, and is said to have murdered his opponents without scruple. When his reign of nearly forty years was drawing near to its close, and conscience was smiting him for his misdeeds, he thought the erection of a monastery would enable him to atone for the crimes he had committed, and that thus he should secure the prayers of religious men for the benefit of his soul after death. While at Bath, he dreamed that an angel appeared to him in the night, and admonished him to raise out of the earth the body of the martyr, St. Alban, and place it in a shrine, with suitable ornament and honour. He accordingly, after much preparation, in the year 791 founded a church on the spot where the martyr's remains were said to have been discovered, and bestowed ample possessions upon the abbot and convent, to whose care he committed the relics and the fabric. He made Willegod the first abbot—a man who had devoted himself to a religious life, and who had been present at the finding of the body. Willegod was succeeded by other ecclesiastics in due order.

The erection of an abbey was followed by the gradual growth of population in the locality. Houses clustered round the new church and buildings, and a village was thus formed, distinct from the ancient site of Verulamium. The sixth abbot of St. Alban's, named Ultinus, being a man of conspicuous activity in all temporal as well as spiritual concerns, invited and encouraged the inhabitants of adjacent parts to build and settle in the town—gave them materials and money to enable them to do so—and laid out and embellished a place for a market. He also built two churches for the use of settlers, at each entrance to the new town, which then became known as St. Alban's, in reference to its situation near to the abbey. This took place in the reign of Edred, about one hundred and fifty years after the date of the foundation of the fabric.

Thus originated and fostered, the place became more populous, and the area of the ancient city served as a quarry, whence the abbots carted away the foundations, arches, and columns of the former structures of Verulamium, and used the materials in the construction of additional buildings in connection with their church and the town. Ealdred the eighth abbot, Eadmer the ninth, and Leofric the tenth, also pursued this course, in the latter part of the tenth and the beginning of the eleventh centuries. Of Eadmer it is recorded that he amassed a vast quantity of the Roman tile, stone, and timber; and that the workmen he employed overturned the remains of a large palace in searching the ruins of the old city. But of the new town little if anything is known, until we hear of it through the Doomsday Survey.

At that time, it was apparently a dependency upon the abbey, though it was called a borough. It contained 46 householders and 12 cottagers; the former possessing half a hide of land. There were tolls and other rents, estimated in the money of the period at £11 13s. yearly value; probably raised from the householders, who were the burgesses of the nascent borough, and who had either inherited or acquired a certain measure of self-government in relation to civil and criminal administration; though no Merchant Guild ever appears to have been established.

On the conquest of the country by the Normans, abbots of the Norman race were substituted for the Saxon ecclesiastics, and they ruled with a heavy hand the townspeople of St. Alban's. Paul was the first of these; he was a relative of Lanfranc, the archbishop of Canterbury. His successor was Rufus, the fifteenth abbot, who extorted money from the tenants of the abbey and the inhabitants of the town.

For a century and a half, however, the townspeople sink below the surface of history; and it is only in a very humble way that they raise their heads above it; but it is in a way characteristic of the English people—it is as complainants against an interference with their practical interests, not as champions of any highflown or abstract theories. They had, it appears, been long accustomed to make woollen cloth of the meanest kind; from which manufacture they derived their livelihood. They wished also to full the cloth (that is, to clean and whiten it), and began to employ the town-mills for the purpose, being content to grind their corn at home in small handmills; yet, however advantageous the proposal might have proved to abbot Roger, he would not permit the mills to be used in fulling, and caused his bailiff to seize the handmills. Great confusion ensued, and the town was thrown into a state of discontent and tumult. As Eleanor, the Queen of Henry the Third, was coming to the abbey, the people hoped they might induce her to intercede with the abbot on their behalf; but the cunning ecclesiastic conducted the Queen to her lodgings by a private way, and thus foiled their purpose. One day, while the uproar was going on, Gregory de Stokes, the constable of Hertford Castle, came to the town, with three armed attendants. As at this period the barons' wars were being waged, under the leadership of Simon de Montfort, the town was barricaded at every avenue. The townsmen, pretending that they thought the constable was coming to burn or plunder the place, seized upon him and his men, and cut off their heads, which they fixed upon poles and set up at each entrance to the town. For this offence, the town was condemned to pay a fine of 100 marks, which was instantly raised. Meanwhile, the Queen effected a compromise between the abbot and the townsmen, and peace was obtained, and the mills were restored to their original use. But the quarrel was not to end here, and more was involved in it than is obvious on the first view of the subject: it was the outbreak of a spirit of general resistance to the authority of the monastery, and the inauguration of a movement on behalf of municipal independence.

The grandsons of the townsmen saw the struggle renewed. Their fathers had no doubt told them that the abbots had not always ruled the burgesses as they had done since the Conquest, and that there were days in which, when the Saxon kings reigned in the land, the people enjoyed a larger share of liberty and greater local privileges. Fifty years elapsed before the burgesses revived their pretensions. In the early part of Edward the Second's reign, Hugo was chosen the twenty-seventh abbot of the monastery. He was a handsome, vain, affected man, who gave great feasts and entertainments to the neighbouring gentry, and especially to the ladies—the resort of the latter to his house being (according to the monkish historians) greater than decency allowed or his dignity required. He was subject to many exactions by the barons, and the royal favourites, and therefore had to raise uncommon supplies. In consequence, he too rigidly exacted all the rights which, as a feudal lord, he could in those days demand; and in this way increased his unpopularity with the townsmen. He laboured under the additional disadvantage that the King, like his father (Edward the First), sided with the people, with the view of curbing the power of the Church. But the abbot's difficulties were the townsmen's opportunities.

Hugo had been elected abbot in the year 1308. He had scarcely assumed the mitre before the burgesses of St. Alban's refused to grind at his mills, and provided themselves with handmills. The abbot endeavoured to suppress them. One Robert de Lymbury having set up a handmill, the bailiff had orders to distrain or seize upon the article, and bring away the upper millstone. Lymbury then resisted the bailiff, who forbore to proceed further; but the abbot brought his action against the recusant townsman, who was eventually committed to gaol, whence he was discharged on paying a fine of 20 shillings, and finding securities not to offend again. The abbot prosecuted similar suits against three other townsmen; and they, in revenge, ill-treated a monk and carried away many of the goods from a house in the town belonging to the abbot, and threw down trees and committed other depredations. Great disorders were, in fact, daily practised—these being the evidences of the townsmen's resolve not to submit to the abbot's arbitrary regulations.

While all these things were taking place, Thomas, Earl

of Lancaster and Leicester, was resting in the monastery on his way to London. Afraid that their deeds would be made known to the higher powers by the abbot's communications to the earl, the burgesses promised, through twelve of their principal men, if he would not relate to the earl their various trespasses and offences, they would rectify all disorders and conform to the laws of the land. The abbot, confiding in these promises, complied with their request. No sooner, however, had the earl left the town, than a servant of the abbot was captured and very ill treated; and, still more to show their enmity, the burgesses erected a gallows in the market place, and affixed to it an axe, fastened by a chain, with a written threat appended, that whosoever refused to join in their movement for municipal liberty should be beheaded. Next day, the twelve delegates of the townsmen went to the abbot, claiming certain privileges. At first moderate in their requests, they became more earnest and urgent; and finally, speaking in a high tone, proceeded to menaces. The abbot, after a short consideration, requested them to reduce their demands to writing, to specify them in articles, and to return with them in four days thus formulised. But the twelve townsmen (evidently appreciating their opportunity, and understanding the yielding disposition of the sociable and convivial ecclesiastic with whom they had to negotiate) pressed their pretensions without delay. On the day following, therefore, they visited him again, and presented an indenture containing the articles, demanding an immediate answer.

The articles they presented indicate (as already hinted) that the townsmen retained among them traditions of ancient privileges wrested from them after the Conquest. They were as follow:—

"1. That the community of the town supplicated the "Abbot and Convent that they would yield up to "them their privileges and the charter confirmatory of

"them, as they had ever used and enjoyed them from
"the time of the making of the charter referred to,
"until the last abbot had hindered them in so doing, as
"the charter itself would testify, and as was set forth
"in Doomsday Book, wherein their town was styled
"a 'borough' and they 'burgesses.'
"2. They entreated that leave might be given them to
"choose two burgesses to go to the king's parliament,
"according to the liberty granted to other boroughs,
"and as they themselves had been used to do in times
"past.
"3. They entreated that they might have leave to make
"answer, in all matters of inquisition and pleas before
"the justices itinerant, by twelve men chosen in the
"town, without any admixture of non-residents.
"4. They prayed that the assize of ale and bread might
"be observed and kept by twelve men of their town,
"being burgesses and sworn, as had been accustomed
"in times past.
"5. They prayed that they might have common in the
"lands, woods, waters, fisheries, and other commodities,
"as mentioned in Doomsday, and which they had
"formerly enjoyed.
"6. They prayed to be allowed to have handmills, and
"to be indemnified in the losses they had sustained by
"defending them hitherto.
"7. They prayed, lastly, that the bailiff of the town, who
"was appointed by the abbot, should be sworn, and
"should perform all executions—that is, king's writs—
"without interference by the bailiffs of the liberty."

We may observe that it is clear the townsmen here sought to obtain what they believed to be rights of early origin, and other rights, of which the object was to render them to a considerable extent self-governing and independent of the abbatical control. The grievance relating to the

handmills here sinks into a minor item in their catalogue.
It is also somewhat remarkable that the burgesses ask the
permission of *the monastery* to elect members of parliament;
while it might be presumed the authority to do so would be
vested in the hands of the king, or of the king and the two
houses of parliament jointly.

The abbot received the delegates in the consistory of the
abbey, and gave a ready affirmative to each article by word
of mouth; but they, perceiving that this was merely an
evasive way of answering their petitions, and that the concessions were not put in writing (as they had demanded),
left the place in great anger, and returned to the town to
consult with their confederates. The interview took place
on the 21st of January, about one o'clock; and about six
o'clock, when the dark evening had arrived, the townsmen,
on horse and on foot, began a regular assault upon the
abbey, approaching at one of the gates. They raised a great
noise, cast large stones at the abbey portal, and began to
set it on fire. The abbot, meanwhile, had foreseen the contingency, and in the morning had introduced within the
abbey precincts his servants, tenants, and dependents, numbering 200, independently of the monks, of whom there
were probably 100; thus furnishing a strong garrison of
defence. For ten days the siege lasted, involving the
necessity of long watchings and much fasting (for the blockade was strictly maintained, and the provisions were distributed very sparingly); but at last the event reached the
ears of the king (Edward the Second), who was then keeping his court at Windsor. Affecting an air of great concern
for this affront done to his church (since he boasted himself
to be its patron), he transmitted a brief to the sheriff of the
county, ordering him to take his forces to the spot, for the
suppression of the insurgents, and to make his proclamation of peace; all rebels who remained after it was read to

be put in prison, there to await further the royal pleasure or displeasure. On the arrival of the sheriff at St. Albans, he read the proclamation publicly; and it produced a visible effect upon the townsmen, for they no longer carried arms or terrified the abbey clergy with hostile demonstrations; but they were only the more bitter with their reproaches and invectives, which they hurled unsparingly at their monkish rulers. They also formed a kind of confederacy with some of the neighbouring towns, and with some of the inhabitants of London; binding themselves to each other by oath, and collecting money in order to engage lawyers to defend them, and to procure their liberties.

The controversy was then conducted in a legal manner, and it would be interesting to the historical student here to present the detailed particulars of its progress; but in this essay it must suffice to state that the result was an agreement of the abbot and convent, forced upon them by the king's letter, that the town should be a borough, and be held as a borough; that all the tenements within the bounds should be "burgesses"; that all the good men in the place, and their heirs and successors, within the said bounds dwelling, should be burgesses, and for burgesses holden for ever; and that they might elect two burgesses to go to every parliament. Twenty-four townsmen were appointed to walk the bounds and define the ancient limits.

They did so, and the area thus marked out constituted the borough. The effect of this change was to empower the inhabitants to elect juries, to appear in a court of their own, called a Leet—not at the abbot's sessions—and to choose their own bailiff. "This effort of the townsmen," very appositely observes the writer from whose work most of these details have been selected,* "was intended to

---

* *History of the Abbey of St. Albans*, by the Rev. P. Newcome, Rector of Shenley, Herts, 1795; compiled from the Chronicles of Matthew of Paris and Walsingham.

detach themselves from the rule and authority of the abbot, and to erect themselves into a degree of corporate capacity for their better government at home, and the furtherance of their business in the great council of the nation." And the rights of the townsmen, which were before vague and undefined, and apparently dependent to a considerable degree on the will of the abbott, were now ascertained and confirmed by charter.

Elated by their success, and intoxicated by their complete triumph over their ecclesiastical lord, the inhabitants committed some excesses. On the day on which possession was given to them of the common of Bernate Heath, they broke down the branches of the beech-trees, and marched back into the town, bearing them on their shoulders as in token of victory; and subsequently they destroyed hedges and fences, hunted hares and rabbits and all the game they could find, in certain woods near St. Alban's, and set up eighty handmills.

This occurred in the year 1327. The townsmen now called themselves "burgesses," and refused to recognise the jurisdiction of the abbot's court and steward within their limits. In this way they continued for three years, until a tragic incident happened, which was the first of a series of circumstances terminating in the entire defeat of the burgesses.

It is alleged that the latter, when they had thrown off the authority of the abbot in all civil matters, refused also to recognise his spiritual authority, and became dishonest and profligate. Probably this charge proceeded from the monks, who, chagrined at their defeat in the recent struggle, meditated revenge, and laid their plans to entrap and embarrass the imprudent townsmen; but whatever may have been the origin of the allegation, the abbot soon found a victim upon whom to visit his displeasure. Among the most conspicuous of the rebellious burgesses was one named Taverner, who was accused of a variety of offences. Two monks and the abbot's marshal, named Amersham, were despatched with a summons to Taverner to appear in the abbot's court. A large crowd assembled to witness the service of the summons, when a violent fray ensued, between the monks and the marshal, on one side, and Taverner and the townspeople (among whom were many women) on the other. In the scuffle, Taverner struck the marshal, and the latter laid his opponent prostrate, never to rise again. The women avenged their townsman's fall by killing the marshal. The crowd hurried away the two summoners, and other persons who had joined them, to the king's coroner, then dwelling in St. Alban's. Measures were immediately taken by the sheriff to secure the appearance of the monks concerned in the fray, and of the abbot, to answer for the death of the two men. A precept was also issued to the sheriff, by the coroner and his companions, requiring him to summon 24 men of the abbey liberties, and 24 men of the town to make inquisition into the affair; but the townsmen refused to be joined with the abbot's men in the proceeding, demurring to their right to interfere. However, the inquisition was instituted, and on the day appointed the burgesses produced the king's writ, commanding the jury to allow them to enjoy their privileges as a borough, and confirming them in their claim to decide respecting all trespasses and felonies occurring in their town by the intervention of their own town jury solely. On the other side, to the great mortification of the inhabitants, the abbot produced the king's writ to liberate the men imprisoned. This document was read aloud in the presence of the jury, and of countrymen present from some of the adjoining hundreds, who loudly applauded the decision—arbitrary as it was—of the king, and rejoiced to see the "upstart consequence of the townsmen taken down," as the history of the transaction relates.

At the end of the ten days, the abbot assumed the offensive again: he indicted the townsmen before the judges, for the death of Amersham and a person named Ely, whom they had killed two or three years before in an affray. They now found themselves unequal to the task of coping with their energetic ecclesiastical adversary, and therefore they proposed a conference, with a view to effect an amiable compromise of their differences. This was attended by many of the principal men of the neighbourhood, on the part of the abbot and convent, and by a citizen of London and a sergeant-at-law, on the part of the burgesses; but the latter pressed their right to use the handmills with such pertinacity that the business made no progress, and it was resolved to proceed against them by bill.

All this took place in the year 1331. In the month of September, the king's judges were expected at Hertford, to hold the assizes there for the county. Before the day arrived on which the judges sat, the abbot provided a cask of wine, and ample materials—meat, fish, and other viands —sufficient for a week's consumption, in order to entertain the judges and the company assembled, at the priory in the county town. Thus entertained by the abbot, the judges heard the case he had prepared against the townsmen, which consisted of charges of cruelty to the servants of the abbey, and similar offences. The accused made no defence; but submitted to be fined, and were compelled to pay the penalties there and then, without leaving the court. They still insisted on their right to have the handmills; but it was in vain, for the judges decided the matter in favour of the abbot. An attempt was then made to effect an arrangement with him; but he was now in the ascendant and refused, unless on such terms as were intolerable to the burgesses.

A year after the death of Amersham, in the month of May, the townsmen felt they were powerless. They went to the abbot and made a voluntary surrender of their charter of liberties, and other charters and records besides. They handed over to him a deed of arbitration made in their favour. They gave up the perambulation of the borough. They took their millstones to the church and there deposited them, in token of renouncing for ever their right of grinding at home, instead of at the abbey mills. They presented to the abbot the town chest and its three keys, as indicating that they gave up all their corporate rights, and abandoned all hopes in future of being a free and independent community. Having thus thrown themselves at the feet of their ecclesiastical superior, and allowed themselves to be once more put in civic fetters, they were invited to dinner at the abbey; and with the fumes of the abbot's wine in their heads, they seem to have forgotten their defeat and their degradation, for they shortly after consented to make a formal renunciation of all the rights, privileges, and immunities which they had obtained from the last abbot, Hugh; thus recording their own civic prostration and downfall, in a way which allowed neither of forgetfulness nor revocation.

Fifty years elapsed without witnessing any attempt on the part of the people of St. Alban's to regain their surrendered privileges. In the reign of Richard II. a spasmodic effort was made by them in this direction, when Wat Tyler and Jack Straw obtained a temporary success; but it ended in failure—not, however, until the young king, accompanied by 1,000 bowmen and soldiers, had been to St. Alban's, with Chief Justice Tressilian, who sentenced three of the townsmen and fifteen other persons to be hanged for rising against the authorities. The sentence was executed; the grants extorted from the abbot during the insurrection were abandoned; and the mill-stones restored to the abbot.

From this time (the year 1382) until the year 1553, the burgesses continued wholly dependent on the abbey; as they had been compelled to become by Abbot Richard, the second abbot of that name. When the Reformation was established, and the religious community of the abbey overthrown, the burgesses were duly incorporated by Edward the Sixth; by whose charter, modified in subsequent reigns and confirmed in that of Charles II., the government was vested in a mayor, high steward, recorder, twelve aldermen, and twenty-four assistants, with a town clerk (who usually acted as chamberlain and coroner), two sergeants at mace, and subordinate officers. This local constitution remained in existence until superseded by the new corporation elected under the new Municipal Reform Act, in 1835.

CHAPTER IV.

THE BOROUGH OF LEICESTER.

A spectator standing on the rising ground to the south and south-east of the modern town of Leicester, sees stretched in the plain below, covering many acres, the red brick dwellings of its eighty thousand inhabitants. Among these rise tall factory chimneys and the towers of the churches, modern and ancient—the latter indicating its size and importance in bygone periods ; the former by their volumes of vapour telling of the manifold agencies which machinery is setting in motion daily for the benefit of a thriving population.

Eighteen centuries ago the scene was far different. All around was a vast forest. Through the valley flowed a small stream, which took its rise a few miles southwards. Sinuous in its course, it made many windings through level banks, and offered sites which a military invader, looking out for one suitable for an encampment, would select as advantageous for defence, and which, perhaps, the natives themselves had already known, from their being protected by the river on two sides, as sheltered quarters for their tempomry settlements. On one of these spots, it is conjectured, Ostorius Scapula, the general of Claudius, or one of his lieutenants, in the campaign which determined the fate of this part of the island, laid out the four sides of a camp, which became afterwards a Roman Station.

Of this place the Museum of Leicester contains many relics ; attesting the extent and greatness of its public buildings, the beauty of the pavements which once formed the floors of its houses, and the variety of its household requisites. Columns of considerable girth, capitals of elaborate sculpture, tesselated fragments of ingenious device. Samian pottery of bright red, the necks and handles of wine-jars, brooches of various kinds, and many other unnamed articles—all the waifs of a past civilization and of a fashion whose grace has departed—speak eloquently of the city whose builders are forgotten, but whose works prove them to have been men of art, and skill, and cunning. Among these remains, also, is one which places beyond question the recognition of Leicester, as Ratæ, by the Romans, and which suggests the presence here of Hadrian, on his tour northwards, in the year 120 A.D. The relic here referred to is a milestone, formerly standing on the road to Lincoln, about two miles northward of the town; the inscription upon which bears a dedication to the emperor just named, and the name of Ratæ and the distance of the stone from the Station. Further illustrating the character of the place, as a centre of authority and population, a large pile of masonry stands on the western side of the town, for many generations known as the Jewry Wall, which recent excavations and enquiries have proved, in the estimation of local antiquaries, to have been the western gateway of Roman Leicester. Beyond this, in the immediate suburbs, lies buried in a field a line of tesselated pavements, formerly those of an extensive villa—doubtless the residence of one of the principal officials of the place in the third or fourth century (as the discovery of coins of a certain period indicates).

Of this abode of a numerous population, History says nothing. Beyond the bare mention of it by Ptolemy, and the insertion of its name on the Roman itineraries, no known written records allude to its existence. Richard of Cirencester (as before stated) classes it among the lowest order of Roman settlements—the Stipendiary Towns—the municipal condition of which was briefly described in the first Chapter. Sharing the lot of its contemporaries, it must in the reign of Caracalla have become an enfranchised city.

E

But here ends all that can be ascertained of Ratæ; except what archæology tells us in the architectural relics remaining above-ground and in others disentombed, and in the household and other fragments above briefly catalogued.

Disappearing from the surface of history as Ratæ, the town re-appears, after a long interval, under another name. The river, on the banks of which it stood, had been designated the Leir, or Leogra, by the Saxons, who had penetrated to the interior of the island and appropriated the district to themselves; and to the place itself they gave the name of Leogra-cester, or Leir-cester—the fortified town on the Leir. Judging from the abject condition to which the Romanized inhabitants, in common with their compatriots elsewhere, had been reduced under the despotic regulations of the emperors—the land having been allowed to remain uncultivated, the towns having been partially deserted, and the inhabitants left behind being famished and spiritless[*]— the Germanic invaders met with little resistance in taking possession. The place first comes into sight again about the year 653, when, it is stated, Penda, king of Mercia (in which state the town was situate), wishing to accomplish the marriage of his son Peada, with the daughter of Oswy, king of Northumberland, took measures for the coronation of Peada in Leircester. It was then known also as the metropolis of the Middle Angles. In the year 679, it became the seat of a bishop, on the division of Mercia into four dioceses by Theodore, Archbishop of Canterbury; and several bishops in succession were here resident.

At this date it was known as a "city." Whether this appellation had simply an ecclesiastical significance,—or whether it had the meaning attaching to its classical derivation—(most probably it had the former)—it was a place of

[*] *History of the Origin of Representative Government in Europe*, by M. Guizot. Bohn's Edition, 1852. Part 1, Lecture 23.

importance, and as such would not, it is presumed, be without municipal franchises. An authority already quoted* informs us, that on the decay of the municipal system, the office of the *Defensor* was instituted, whose mission was to defend the people, especially the poor, against the oppression and injustice of the imperial officers and their agents, and that the bishop (who was appointed the *Defensor*) in this way acquired the chief power in the municipalities.

What kind of local government was in force, in the time of the Mercian monarchs and the Saxon bishops, we are left to conjecture; but whatever it was, it did not remain in unbroken operation, as the irruptions of the Danes, at the close of the ninth century [866 to 900 A.D.] must have thrown all local affairs into confusion. Should the example of Winchester have been followed in Leicester, a Merchant Guild may have been established here at the same time [856 A.D.]; or, what is not improbable, such a society may have been founded, both here and there, long before the recognition by Ethelwulph in his charter of the Guild at Winchester. The conquest of the Danes over the towns-people of Nottingham, Derby, Lincoln, Stamford, and Leicester—the Five Boroughs, as they were called—was, however, an event which was followed by a complete change of masters, and of the internal rule of those towns. In Leicester, the Danes had a long lease of power; and, as in Lincoln and Stamford they established a governing class of magistrates, termed "laghe-men" or "law-men," (whose possession of a "manse," or allotment of land, qualified them to hold the office,) so it is fair to assume they did here likewise.

When we arrive at the reign of Edward the Confessor, a gleam of light falls on the state of the borough. The incidental mention of the payments made then to the crown, recorded in the Doomsday Survey, shows its relationship to

* Guizot's *Representative Government*, Part 1, Lecture 23.

the sovereign authority. "The city of Leicester," says the Survey, "in the time of King Edward paid yearly to the king thirty pounds by tale and sixteen sextaries of honey. When the king marched with his army through the land, twelve burgesses of that borough attended him. If the king went over the sea against the enemy, they sent four horses from that borough as far as London, to convey arms and baggage."

Now, from this brief statement, we deduce the following conclusions :—1. That Leicester was a "borough,"—in other words, a town having an independent local administration, and governed by its own officers—between the years 1042 and 1066, when the Confessor occupied the throne of England. 2. That the king was its ancient lord—not as sovereign of the land, perhaps, but as the representative of its ancient seigniors, in existence before the establishment of the Heptarchy; the Saxon monarchs being sometimes lords of manors, anciently, in the same way as their principal thanes were. 3. That the yearly contribution of money and honey to the king was the price paid to him, as their lord, for exercising an independent jurisdiction : it was the commutation, in truth, of the numerous local payments required by the ancient lords, into one payment, the burgesses enjoying, as a consequence, the right to levy the local burdens among themselves, without interference by the reeves or bailiffs of the king.

We may infer, then, that the organizations before named as requisite for the carrying on of local affairs—the Court Leet for the civil and criminal administration, the Merchants' Guild for the management of municipal matters— were at work among the inhabitants before the Roman Conquest.

This will be seen more fully as we proceed. The readers of national history will have learnt that the Battle of Hastings did not of itself determine the future destiny of

England's government. It will be found that town after town fought its own battle for freedom, as if each were a small republic resolved on maintaining its own separate vitality against the efforts of the invader to ensure its destruction. When William of Normandy set out to confront the hostile assemblages collected against him in the north of England, in the year 1068 A.D., the first place he assaulted was Oxford, the next was Warwick, the next Leicester, and so he proceeded to Derby, Nottingham, and Lincoln—at all of which towns he encountered a vigorous resistance, inspired by the consciousness of the inhabitants that they were independent communities, and unwilling to admit they could not hold their own against the attack of the foreigner.

The Conquest did not occasion the overthrow of the Merchants' Guild in Leicester; as we may feel certain that it did not originate with the Norman Duke or his barons. They found it in existence in the place and they permitted its continuance.

We may here remark that it was once the fashion of a school of historical enquirers to assume that the charters of the lords of the English towns created the boroughs, and conferred on the burgesses, as something novel, the rights and privileges they detailed; but fuller investigation has proved that those rights and privileges had an imprescriptive antiquity, and that the charters were merely guarantees on parchment of the good faith with which the lords would observe and maintain the long-established usages—in return for a considerable pecuniary acknowledgment.

After the townsmen of Leicester had succumbed to the troops of William's Norman army, they and their property were divided up among some of his chief friends and military associates. The King had his rents and a certain portion of the houses of the subjugated inhabitants, and the

Archbishop of York, Hugh de Witwile, Robert de Veasy, Goisfrid de Wirce, Henry de Ferrers, Robert the King's Steward, and the Countess Judith, had their shares in the spoliation; but the principal on the list was Hugh de Greutmesnil, who became Earl of Leicester—a personage who, in the year in which the siege of the town occurred, was of the number of those who returned to their wives and children in Normandy, deserting his duty as a vassal to watch over his honour as a husband. His successor was Robert de Mellent, the favourite of Henry, the Conqueror's son, and a man distinguished by his hatred of the native English, but who, nevertheless, granted a charter to the men of Leicester, which leaves no doubt of the existence of their Merchant Guild within twenty years after the capture of their town. Here is a translation of the document*:—

"Robert, Earl of Mellent, to Ralph, and all his barons,
"French and English, of all his land in England,
"greeting. Know ye that I have granted to my
"merchants of Leicester their Guild Merchant with all
"customs which they held in the time of King William,
"King William his son, and now hold in the time of
"Henry the King. Witness, R the son of Alcitil."

The obtainment of this charter, as the first grant they sought at the hands of their Norman lord—who, it may be observed, here holds a position of sovereignty over them— implies that the Merchants' Guild was indispensable to the inhabitants; that with it they had enjoyed certain other "customs;" and that the Conquest, severe as was its shock, had not stopped the proceedings of the Guild—that is, if it had pre-existed, as, looking at the examples afforded by other towns, it had done undoubtedly.

* The Charter itself is not extant; but a copy is preserved in an ancient vellum book, now preserved in the Muniment Room in Leicester, entitled "*Borough Charters, Laws of the Portmanmote, &c.*," page 68.

With the Conquerors, among other usages, was brought the trial by battle. Anciently, as we have seen, in the Court Leet were decided the suits of a civil nature arising among the inhabitants, and to this court they appear to have given the name Portmanmote, which rendered into modern English means Townman-meeting—the term "port" being the equivalent of "town" in such words as "port-reeve," "port-meadow," and others. When, therefore, two burgesses had a dispute regarding any right to property, or of a similar kind, in the times prior to the Norman invasion, they carried their case before the Portmanmote, and there, before a sworn tribunal composed of twenty-four of their neighbours, their statements were heard and an award was given. But the Conquerors introduced the principle of duelling, instead of the decision by jurors. Under the Normans the two litigant burgesses, armed with long staves, and bare-headed and bare-legged, were required to fight until one cried craven or was killed. A circumstance occurred in Leicester, in connection with this brutal custom, which led to its abandonment and the revival of the ancient usage, and which is thus described in a document still extant*:—" In the time of Robert the Medland, then earl of Leicester, it happened that two kinsmen, namely, Nicholas the son of Acon, and Geoffrey the son of Nicholas, waged a duel about a certain piece of land, concerning which a dispute had arisen between them ; and they fought from the first to the ninth hour and longer, each conquering by turns, one of them fleeing from the other until he came to a certain little pit; and, as he stood above the pit, and was about to fall therein, his kinsman said to him, 'Take care of the pit—turn back, lest thou should'st fall into it !' And as he stood over the pit, so much clamour and tumult

* Inquisition taken in Leicester, before Roger of Arden, bailiff, Peter Fitz Roger, Mayor, and others, in the 39th of Henry III.

was made by the bystanders, and those who were sitting around, that the earl heard their clamour as far off as the Castle, and he enquired of some of them how it was there was such a clamour; and answer was made to him that two kinsmen were fighting about a certain piece of land, and that one had fled until he reached a certain little pit, and that as he stood over the pit and was about to fall into it, the other warned him. The burgesses, being moved by piety, then made a covenant with the earl that they should give him threepence yearly for each house in the High Street that had a gable, on condition that he should grant to them that the twenty-four jurors, who were in Leicester from ancient times, should from that time forward discuss and decide all pleas they might have among themselves; and this was conceded to them by the earl, and in such manner were the pennies, called gavel-pennies, first levied."

The return to the Portmanmote and its authority was thus confirmed by the charter of earl Robert.

At the time in which these events were happening, the Forest of Leicester extended close up to its western and northern gateways. It was of wide extent, the boughs of its trees were thick and full, and it was at times impassable; its pathways being blocked up by the dead wood and the branches, which, torn off by tempest-blasts, lay scattered in every direction.* The poor inhabitants, in an age when coal was unknown, often felt in their wretched huts the chill cold and frosty wind, without having the means to purchase fuel; and even the well-to-do had need of an abundant supply. At the instance of the inhabitants, therefore, Earl Robert de Mellent granted permission to gather the dead wood to all who pleased, on these conditions: —To pay to the earl for six cart-loads a denier (7½d.), for a

* Ibid.

horse-load weekly one penny, and for a man's load weekly a farthing. At first, the money was collected near to an outlet from the Forest; then, nearer the town; and, lastly, near the bridges. The collector, named Penbrioch, having petitioned the earl to grant him a piece of ground near one of the gates, to build upon, was provided with it, and there he received the wood-money, or bridge-silver, as it was called, from being collected near the bridges. But Penbrioch, not content with receiving the payments for the dead wood, sold the green wood, and appropriated the customs or levies to himself.

Robert de Mellent was succeeded in the year 1118 by his son Robert, surnamed Le Bossu, or the Hunchbacked. Whether it was that he felt disposed gratuitously to abandon the tax, called "gable pennies," imposed in the manner above described, or that he relinquished their enforcement on receipt of a composition in lieu of them, does not appear; but it is on record that he quitted his claim to them for ever. In addition to this he granted the following charter:

"Robert, Earl of Leicester, to Ralph, his deputy, and all
"his barons and men, French and English, health!
"Know ye that I both will and grant to my burgesses
"of Leicester, that they shall hold all their customs,
"well and in peace, both honorably and quietly, in
"their Guild and in all other customs, so that they
"may hold them better, more quietly, and more
"honourably than they ever held them of my father,
"Witnesses: Ernald Dubois, Geoffrey the Abbot,
"Ralph junior, John de Ivi, Matthew de Villiers.
"Baldwin de Charnwood, Ralph the Great [*multum* in
"original], Anifred the son of Alsy, Roger de Crafort,
"Robert the Chaplain."*

* This charter is preserved in the Muniment Room of the Borough of Leicester.

Here, again, the reader will notice that the Guild is regarded as the specific institution which the townsmen most highly estimated. They are here styled "burgesses," not "merchants," as in the first charter, and the earl promises additional security to them in the observance of their customs, which unquestionably included the Portmanmote.

These charters, however, seem not always to have been respected, even by the officers of the feudal baron himself, who not unfrequently offered vexatious interference with the poor townsmen; so that they found it necessary not only to renew these guarantees on the accession of a new earl, but also to secure the definition of their privileges in plainer terms even than before. It was found expedient therefore, even in respect to the permission to gather wood in the Forest of Leicester, to have the concession stated as explicitly as in the following:—

"Robert, Earl of Leicester, to all his stewards, his bailiffs, "and his foresters of the Forest of Leicester, greeting. "I grant to my burgesses of Leicester that it shall be "lawful to them to go in the woods of the neighbour-"hood wheresoever they will for wood, brushwood "for fences, and other necessary things, and to have "free and quiet roads through my forest. That is to "say, by the gate of Deresford and by Holengate as far "as their houses, *still better and more freely than before* "*they had them in the time of my father*, and as the "charter which they have of my father testifies, and "*none of my foresters and servants shall disturb either* "*their men or their waggons or their horseloads*. Wit-"nesses: Master Hugh the Clerk, Simeon the Clerk, "Ralph Friday, Ralph de Martivall, Simon Sorel, "Richard Fitz-Warren."

Among other rights of remote antiquity possessed by townsmen were those of pasturage, and they may be dated prior to the Norman Conquest—if not in the period of the Roman occupation. It was, in truth, essential to the semi-agricultural pursuits of the Leicester burgesses that they should have rights of common on the land round their town for their horses and cattle; and perhaps the only difference in this respect before and after the Conquest was, that in the one period these rights were enjoyed without payment, but that in the other the Norman barons imposed a tax on the townspeople who "turned in" to the Pasture. Here is a charter attributed to Robert le Bossu, having reference to the matter :

"Know all men, present and to come, that I Robert,
"Earl of Leicester, have given, granted, and by this
"present charter confirmed, to the free burgesses of
"the town of Leicester, certain existing bounds, as
"decided and measured by the view of legal men of
"my council, in which I have assigned a certain pas-
"turage which is called Cowhay, beyond the South
"Gates, with free ingress and egress through my
"domain to the said pasturage belonging, that is to
"say, the pasture which lies between my pasture
"which is called Oxhay, near the mill of Amaury
"Danett on the one part, and Tackholme on the other
"part, to have and to hold with its said appurtenances
"to my said burgesses, and their heirs and assigns,
"of me and my heirs, freely, quietly, and for ever
"honourably, by paying to me and my heirs or
"successors for each cow agisted or to be agisted, and
"for all horses in the said pasture agisted or to be
"agisted, three pennies per annum. For this conces-
"sion and confirmation the said burgesses have given
"to me, with their hands, a certain sum of money,
"that neither I, the said Robert, nor my heirs, nor
"successors, nor any person for us or by us, shall

"have any challenge or claim to the said pasture in
"future. In testimony of which I have corroborated
"this charter by my seal. These being witnesses:
"William de Senville, Thomas Esterling, Ralph Marti-
"vall, Ernald Dubois, Gilbert Miners, Geoffrey de
"Craunford, Henry Costeyn, William Tasch, Simon
"Curlevach, John ——, and others."

Robert le Bossu dying in 1167 was succeeded in the earldom by his son, commonly designated Robert Blanchmains, or White Hands. Under his rule the burgesses continued in possession of the customs and immunities their ancestors had obtained from his father and grandfather. They obtained from him a confirmatory grant of their Guild Merchant and all other customs. Being dated at Breteuil, where the Earl lived during a considerable period, the following charter is ascribed to him:—

"Robert, Earl of Leicester, to his under-sheriff, and to all
"his justices and ministers of Leicester, French and
"English, greeting. Know ye that I, to all my bur-
"gesses of Leicester, and to all them that in their
"company will hold themselves, grant to hold of me,
"freely and quietly, with all their customs and all
"things thereto pertaining, their hundred and heriots,
"and that by their payments accustomed and also by
"the increment of £8; so that neither by plea nor for
"any custom they go out of Leicester, but only to the
"Conmecherchie, as of old time was accustomed. I
"grant also to them to hold their Merchant Guild as
"they ever best held it in the time of my father.
"Witness, R. the Primate, and Richard the Master,
"and Baldwin of Greutmesnil, and Barnard the
"Primate. At Breteuil."

When Eleanor, the queen of Henry II. conspired with her sons against her husband, this Earl took part in the unnatural contest against his sovereign. Henry accordingly despatched his Chief Justiciary to the town, and laid it under siege. A fire taking place within the walls compelled the inhabitants to capitulate, and on payment of three hundred pounds of silver they were allowed to leave their homes and seek refuge at St. Edmund's Bury and St. Alban's, where they believed they would enjoy the protection of the two martyr-saints; especially of St. Edmund, who was supposed to be ever willing to protect all men of English race from the tyranny of foreigners. The walls having been destroyed as well as the dwellings consumed by fire, the town became accordingly depopulated and deserted.

How long this scene of desolation may have continued, history does not precisely define; though indications are not wanting that it lasted for about fifteen years. The Earl prepared for a pilgrimage to Jerusalem in the year 1190, and it is supposed at this time confirmed his charters to the burgesses. Dying before he reached the Holy Land, however, his son, called Robert Fitzparnel, inherited the earldom in that year.

Though they had their Merchant Guild and their Portmanmote, or "Conmecherchy" (as it is called in Blanchmain's charter), and therefore were exempt from external interference in respect to their town affairs, the burgesses had been long in a semi-servile condition. They had been compelled to reap the corn crops of the earl, and they were bound to take their wheat to be ground at the Castle Mill; and if their cows or oxen strayed beyond the common in which they had a right of pasturage, into the earl's inclosures where his crops were growing, the earl's officers impounded them and levied a penalty on the owners. As almost every inhabitant probably owned a cow, and some grew small crops of their own on allotments, they felt the regulations imposed by the earl's servants to be irksome and oppressive. These had, in the first instance, very likely originated immediately after the Conquest; but the townspeople avoided the compulsory labour in the fields, by paying a few pence each to the earl's servants, and they sent their wheat to other mills than the earl's on submitting to a tax on every cartload taken elsewhere. Still, they felt these imposts to be troublesome and vexatious, and collisions would often occur in consequence with the myrmidons of the lord of the adjoining castle. It seems to have been the policy of the inhabitants to secure the favour of a new earl immediately on his accession, by asking for a charter and paying a considerable fee for it; and in the case of Robert Fitzparnel, they sought to free themselves, once and for ever, from the degrading liabilities above enumerated. They therefore procured this charter:—

"Robert, Earl of Leicester, son of Petronilla the Countess, to all by whom the present writing may be inspected, greeting! Let it be universally known that, for the health of my soul, and of the souls of my ancestors and successors, I have demised and in every way quit-claimed from me and my heirs for ever those pennies which were accustomed to be taken yearly from my burgesses of Leicester, on account of reaping my corn at Leicester, and at the same time those pennies which were accustomed to be taken from all cows escaping into my enclosure, and at the same time those pennies which were accustomed to be taken from carts carrying corn at Leicester to any other mill than to my mills at Leicester. And that this present writing shall have confirmation hereafter, I have testified by the apposition of my seal. Witnesses: Paul, Abbot of Leicester, Richard, the Cellarer of Lira, and many others."*

Up to this period, the burgesses of Leicester obtained from the lords of the Castle the privileges and liberties they

* See *Borough Charters, Laws of the Portmanmote*, &c., p. 69.

desired, and the charters embodying them indicate what were those which they most urgently required and most dearly cherished. Their Merchants' Guild and their Portmanmote—their union for municipal purposes, and their simple town-court for the adjustment of their occasional differences or grievances—constituted obviously the institutions which were indispensible to their security and welfare. Of the other customs for which they stipulated, a knowledge has also been supplied by the charters; wherein the right to gather wood in Leicester Forest, the right to settle by peaceable arbitrement instead of armed conflict their disputes, and the permission to procure exemption by payments in money from servile field-labours, are shown to be the objects they regard to be of most pressing importance next in order after their Guild and their "Conmecherchie."

When John ascended the throne, the burgesses felt themselves under the necessity of procuring the royal sanction and protection for some of their usages. In the first year of that monarch's reign, when he was at Peterborough (on the 26th of December, 1199,) they solicited him to grant two charters to them. It has been perceived, so far, that the townsmen confined their attention to their internal affairs; but as they periodically travelled from Leicester to other places to sell their merchandize—the cloth they wove or the wool they spun—they were continually liable to obstructions and exactions wherever they went, and therefore they needed the king's authority to resist them successfully. Their external policy was incomplete until they could travel freely, and armed with a warrant to resist the unjust imposts attempted to be inflicted on them in their journeys. They therefore procured a charter from John, granting that they should go and return, freely and without impediment, throughout the whole land, with all their goods and merchandize, reserving to the king and others all those customs or payments which were just and due. The second charter related to sales and purchases of land, which John conceded should be and remain stable and binding if they were made and enrolled in the Court of Portmanmote.

These and similar documents are sometimes attributed to king John's purpose to "incorporate the boroughs;" while in reality they are only confirmations of pre-existing rights, and guarantees to struggling citizens that lawless force and arbitrary power should not molest them in the pursuit of their humble but useful callings.

CHAPTER V.

BOROUGH OF LEICESTER (CONTINUED).

From the constant mention made of the Guild Merchant in the charters, and the place it occupied in the estimation of the burgesses of Leicester, its nature and operations become subjects of interest; while a minute description of its constitution, as far as documentary materials will allow, will, it is presumed, prove acceptable to the historical enquirer, and illustrate the theme of this essay. It will at the same time incidentally afford glimpses into medieval town life, which are as curious as they are unusual.

A meeting of the Guild was originally known in the rolls by the name "morwenspeche," which is traceable to the ancient term "morgenspræc," employed to designate the "morning speeches," or heathen festivals, of primeval Germany, from which the subsequent meetings of Anglo-Saxon England may be supposed to have been derived.[*] As every consultation was connected with a convivial feast among the early Germans, and a common building was constructed in which the rude banquets and deliberations of the less wealthy freemen were held, the name of which (*domus conviviæ*) implied thus much, so their descendants in this country appear to have introduced the "morwenspeche" and the Guild Hall with their other customs. In Leicester the entries on the Guild, introducing the matters recorded, sometimes commence in this style: "Hec est le morwenspeche de la Gild," thus intermingling Latin, German, and French in the same sentence; the writer being unable to substitute for the words "morwenspeche" and "Gild" any French or Latin equivalents, and thereby unconsciously proving their Teutonic origin.

[*] Lappenberg's *History of England under the Anglo-Saxon Kings*.

We learn from the rolls of the Guild Merchant of Leicester* that usually once a year the members met in their Hall to admit new members and to transact other business. At their head sat the Alderman, or Aldermen; for sometimes one person is mentioned, sometimes two are noticed. The custom was to require the initiate to take an oath of fealty to the Guild; to find two pledges or securities for the fulfilment of his obligations; to pay a fee on entrance, a contribution for the bull, a payment to the "hanse," and smaller ones not specified. Having complied with these requirements, the new member was called a brother of the Guild, was entitled to enjoy all its advantages, was liable to discharge all its corresponding responsibilities, and was eligible to fill its offices. The oath which the new member was required to take was administered in Norman-French, and ran in these terms :†

> "This hear you, Mayor and Brethren of the Guild, that I
> "lawfully the laws of the Guild will keep, and my
> "Guild in all things will follow, whether among my
> "brethren of the Guild or whether I scot in the
> "Bishop's Fee. And that I will warn my Mayor and
> "the good people of the commune if I know of any
> "man who merchandizes in the franchise who may be
> "able to enter the Guild. And that I shall be obedient
> "and observant of the commands of the Mayor and

* These documents are in part preserved in the Town Museum, and in part in the Muniment Room of the Borough.

† The following formula is copied from the vellum book of *Borough Charters, Laws of Portmanmote*, &c. "Le serment de ceux q' entrunt la Gylde. Ceo oyetz vo' meyr et vos freres de la Gylde que ieo leaument les leys de la Gylde tendray, et ma Gylde bien en totes eschoses sucray, et ou mes freres de la Gylde ou que ieo soye escoteray sur le fee l'Evesque. . . . . Et que ieo garniray mon mair et le bone gentz de la commune si ieo sache nul homo que marchaunde deins la fraunchise soit able dentrer la Gylde. Et que ieo serray obedient et servaunt al comandement del mair et ses somounes, et les fraunchises et les bones custum es de la vile a mon poer moynteneray. Si deux me aydo et ses soyns. Amen."

"his summons, and the franchises and the good cus-
"toms of the town according to my power I will
"maintain. So God and his saints help me! Amen."
The nature of the oath shows what the members of the
Guild deemed to be the obligations of one to the other.
First, the new member pledged himself to keep the laws
of the body, whether he lived in the town or the Bishop's
Fee—a district immediately outside the walls, under a jurisdiction independent in some respects of the borough, the
residents of which enjoyed, to a certain extent, the advantages of protection by the town and of their contiguity to
it, without bearing their share of the public burdens.
Secondly, the new member promised to inform the Mayor
of any person living in the town and carrying on trade,
who avoided the incidents of Guild fellowship, while avail-
ing himself of the benefits of Guild arrangements. Thirdly,
the said new member bound himself to abide by the regulations of the society into which he had entered, and to
obey its chief officer, who is here called the Mayor, but who
was in the first instance designated the Alderman.

The formula of admission is recorded on the Guild Roll
in the manner exemplified by a few out of thousands of
instances:

"Peter, the blacksmith, is quit of entrance fee, of the
hanse, and of the bull."*

"Roger of Kibworth is quit of entrance fee, of the bull,
of the hanse, and of everything."†

"William of Thurkill, found pledges, and is discharged
of everything for 4s."‡

* *Petrus ferrator q't de introitu et de ha's et de tauro.*

† *Rog 'de Kibworthe q't de introitu et de tauro et de ha's et de om'ibus' rebs.*

‡ *Will of Thurkill inven. pleg. qt de om̃ib's p. iiii.*

"Peter the nephew of Oliver; pledges, Alan the nephew of Oliver, and Robert the nephew of Oliver, and he is discharged of all things."*

In the case of most of the novitiates who paid the demands upon them, pledges or securities are not mentioned; but in the other cases invariably, where the record does not note the payment of the demands, the names of the securities are inscribed on the roll. The entrance-fee is of course considered an equivalent for permission to join the Guild; and the payment for the bull will be well understood, when it is remembered that many of the members of the Guild depastured cows on the common near the town; while the contribution to the hanse seems only to relate to the periodical subscription to the Guild—the word "hanse" and the word "guild" being synonymous.† When the son of a member of the Guild was admitted, it was under favourable circumstances; he was said to have "the seat of his father," and no payments were required. Thus:—

"Ralph son of Jocelyn has the seat of his father."

"Simon with the beard has the seat of his father."‡

In the case of the servants of members of the Guild, a similar freedom from fees appears to have been occasionally allowed, as is here exemplified:

"Geoffrey, the man of Osmond the Tailor, is quit of entrance-fee."

The son of a priest was placed in a similar position——*Osmond filius sacerdotis* being admitted without payment of fees.

---

* *Petrus nepos Oliveri, plegii Alan. nepos Oliveri, Rob. nepos Oliveri, quietus de omnibus rebus.*

† "*Hanse*: a Company, Society, or Corporation of Merchants." *Old Dictionary.*

‡ *Rad. f Jocelin ht. sedem patris sui.—Sim. cum barba ht. sedem patris sui.*

Finally, concerning the members of the Guild, it may be remarked that they constituted the "burgesses" of the town, and none other.

Originally, the chief officer of the Guild was the Alderman, who was sometimes associated with a colleague. It is not clear whether he was elected by the brotherhood or by the earl; though it is probable by the former, subject to the veto of the latter. In the ancient rolls, one of the days on which the Guild assembled is thus headed:

"These entered the Guild Merchant on the Thursday next after the Purification of the Blessed Mary, in the tenth year of the reign of King John [1209], before William Fitz-Leviric, the Alderman of the Guild."

Another entry on the rolls is as follows:

"These entered the Guild Merchant at the Feast of the Apostles Philip and James, in the fifteenth year of King John [May, 1214], in the time of William Fitz-Leviric, Alderman."

A further entry on the roll presents an example of two Aldermen:

"These entered the Guild on the Thursday before the Annunciation of the Blessed Mary, in the time of Simon Curlevache and John Fitz-Warren, Aldermen of the Guild, in the year next after the death of William Pepin, Abbot of Leicester [1226]."

A fourth entry on the roll repeats the names of the two aldermen. On another occasion, Simon Curlevache's name only appears as that of the presiding alderman.

In the eighteenth year of King Henry the Third it is distinctly stated that William of St. Lo was elected an alderman, to act in conjunction with Simon Curlevache, and it is the first case of the kind mentioned on the records; although the practice was possibly usual in all previous instances. In the year 1251, the term "Alderman" was disused, and the word "Mayor" substituted uniformly for it, and only one officer, thus designated, presided over the Guild meetings.

It was not until the close of King John's reign [1214-1215] that the chief officer of London was styled the Mayor, a charter of that monarch having empowered the "Barons" of the metropolis—otherwise Aldermen—to choose a Mayor from among themselves yearly. We infer that the term was derived from France, from the circumstance of finding it employed in the charters of Beauvais and St. Quentin, as early as about the years 1100 and 1102. In the former of these, this clause occurs : "Thirteen peers shall be elected by the commune, from whom, after the vote of other peers and of all those who shall have sworn to the commune, one or two shall be created Mayors [*majeurs*]."*

The municipal system of Laon was based in part upon the model of Noyon—in part upon that of St. Quentin; and there "the administration of justice and of the public policy was confided to a *major* or mayor, and to elective jurors, of whom the number was twelve at least."†

It is to be presumed that the real meaning of the term was taken from the Latin word *Major*, pronounced *Mayor*, signifying the greater of the aldermen—the one who had the superior position from seniority of appointment or the greater importance of the functions he fulfilled. Whatever may have been the derivation of the term, however, it is placed beyond doubt that the Mayor in Leicester finally acted without a colleague, and was invariably known as the "Mayor of the Guild." The importance of the office in the estimation of the Norman lords of the place is demonstrated by the fact that some of the first aldermen or mayors were of Norman origin, and members of the earl's council, whose names appear as witnesses to the charters granted by the

* *Lettres sur l'Histoire de France*, by Aug. Thierry, 2d. ed. p. 297.
† Ibid, p. 310.

earls to the burgesses; while the surnames of others indicate the truth of the statement. The name of Simon Curlevache, for instance, is among the witnesses to a charter of the Countess Petronilla and another ascribed to Robert Blanchmains; the surnames Fitz-Leviric, Fitz-Warren, Fitz-Roger, and St. Lo, unequivocally indicating a Norman extraction. It has been perceived by the oath taken by the members of the Guild, that they were bound to show obedience to the commandments and summonses of the Mayor, and therefore he held a position of supreme control over the body.

A portion of the Guild members was, however, chosen to advise with the Alderman or Mayor, and to constitute his Council. During Simon Curlevache's aldermanship (from 1225 to 1239), the first election of the Council is recorded to have taken place, though it must have occurred yearly, as a matter of course, without being mentioned on the roll. It is thus noticed:

"These were elected for the common council of the Guild, "to come to all summonses of the Alderman to counsel "with him about the town, and to follow him in the "affairs of the town as his posse, if they are in the "town, under a penalty of 6d. :—Simon Curlevache, "alderman, John Fitz-Geoffrey, Walter of the Grave-"yard, Peter Caufok, Walter le Viccar, Henry Swann, "William le Blund, Robert Warren, Simon Turk, "Philip Fitz-Robert, Reginald Whatborough, William "Morel, Martin Kage, Simon Keling, Simon Swann, "Henry Costeyn, Richard Ratin, Willard, William of St. "Lo, Lawrence Fitz-Ralph, Peter Fitz-Ralph, William "Baldwin, John Fitz-Roger, Peter Ediman, Ralph of "Swepston."*

* The words of the entry are these: Isti electi sunt pro communem consilium Gilde ad veniend' ad omnes summoniciones aldermanni ad consulendum villam et ad eum sequendum negociis ville pro posse suo si sint in villa, sub pena vi d," and so on.

Here are twenty-four names of burgesses of the upper class and probably of Norman origin, to whom, with the Alderman at their head, was entrusted the management of the town business, during the year for which they were elected to serve. Among the number was one William of St. Lo, commonly called Senlo—who in the year 1233 was joint alderman with Simon Curlevache. What was the nature of their duties has in part been described in the record of their appointment; but the oath they took, and the taking of which constituted them "Jurrets" (Jurats), or sworn men, evidences fully what functions they were required to exercise:

> "This hear ye, Mayor, Jurats, and Brethren of the Guild,
> "that I lawful judgments will render, and lawfully
> "will do, as well to the poor as the rich, according to
> "the quantity of their trespass, and that I will come
> "continually to the Court of Portmote, and to the
> "summons of my mayor. That I will be warned by
> "the Bailiff when I may be in the town, if I have no
> "reasonable excuse. And that I will lawfully main-
> "tain the assize of bread, wine, and beer with the
> "mayor. And the franchises, and the good customs
> "of the town will maintain and keep according to my
> "power. So may God and his Saints help me!"

In this oath (though that sworn a century later, perhaps, than at the date to which these explanations chiefly refer) it may be discovered that the Common Council of the Guild was composed of Jurats *(Jurati)*, who were magistrates and assessors with the Mayor in the Portmanmote, and authorised to fix the prices of bread, wine, and beer, as well as to assist the chief magistrate in the execution of his duty generally. It does not appear that the power of life and death over their fellow-burgesses was vested in the Mayor and Jurats; and it is more likely that in such extreme instances the Steward of the Earl, or the Earl himself, sitting in the Castle, pronounced sentence of death upon offenders upon whom it was considered lawful to inflict capital punishment.

Besides the Mayor and Council of the Guild, other subordinate functionaries were required. Where contributions are periodically paid, the task of receiving the amounts and accounting for them will necessarily devolve upon some one or more trustworthy persons. In this way Receivers or Chamberlains of the Guild came to be appointed. In the Rolls of the year 1204-5, the names of Robert Brun and Robert Blund are given as those of persons to whom the entrance-fees and other payments were to be made; in the year 1210 Richard Pilfe and Geoffrey Ordriz are styled "receivers"; and in 1216 Roger de Carleton and Eustace Freebody are designated "Chamberlains of the receipts." As the Guild acquired additional property and importance, regulations were made affecting the position and duties of these officers.

In the times to which allusion is here made, the drawing up of the rolls themselves required the services of a clerk, who was sometimes called the "Mayor's clerk," and who, in addition to being present at the Guild meetings and there enrolling the names of new members, kept an account of the receipts and expenses of the body, entered originally on the back of the skin on which the names were inserted.

A still more humble functionary remains to be named. It must be obvious that some kind of public notice was necessary of all meetings of the Guild; and as neither writing nor printing was available in the centuries here referred to, the burgesses were convened by the ringing of a handbell. It is recorded on an early roll that "the bell was bought in the morwenspech in the vigils of St. Mark the Evangelist for 6d. of Richard Cook, by order of the

Guild, and was transferred to the hands of Adam of Winchester, in the year in which the city of Damietta was taken by the Christians." It was also subsequently transferred to Roger le Wruett. These were the earliest known bellmen of the Guild—Adam of Winchester and Roger le Wruett.

The jurisdiction of the Guild appears to have been indefinite and varying. It had, however, the power to fine, and in case of need to expel members who violated its laws; and sometimes it placed offenders under its bann. The earliest example of fining on record is given in relation to a list of defaulters, of whom it is stated that they are to pay at the next "morwenspech"—if they pay they will be quit—if not, they will be adjudged to pay a tun of beer each. In other cases, fraudulent transactions in trade, and quarrelsomeness were punished by penalties, and a measure of beer was the common form in which the fine was paid. Expulsion was very rarely resorted to by the Guild, and then only as the last possible extremity to which it proceeded. About the year 1212, Osborn of Weston, Geoffrey the groom, and a third person, were placed under the ban of the Guild—were, it may be presumed, suspended for a time in the enjoyment of its privileges.

After this examination of the composition of the Guild, and of the powers and functions of its officers, in the reigns of Richard I., John, and the early part of Henry III., we may return to the history of the charters obtained subsequently to the date in which Robert Fitz-Parnel, the last of the line of Norman barons, possessed the earldom.

As that personage left no issue, the representatives of his honours were his two sisters, Amicia, married to Simon de Montfort, and Margaret, the wife of Saher de Quincy. The earldom of Leicester descended to the former, who is known in history as the chief of the sanguinary crusades against

the Albigenses; but his connection with the place is not
associated with any concession or confirmation of privileges
or liberties. Between the years 1207 and 1218, in which he
was in possession of the earldom, with intervals in which
the tenure was broken, he was generally engaged in military
enterprises in France. After his death at the siege of
Toulouse, he was succeeded in his local honours by his
fourth son, Simon, the more celebrated baron, whose name
is inseparably identified with the origination of the parliamentary system of England.

By this earl several charters were granted to the
burgesses of Leicester, of which mention may be here
introduced. At this time, the Guild and the Portmanmote
had probably been established too long and too firmly to
need confirmation by the lords of the town; and hence we
no longer meet with charters in which they are further
guaranteed. But the right to pasturage in the Cow-hay was
secured by a charter of renewal from Simon de Montfort.
A circumstance occurred also, about the middle of the long
term during which Simon de Montfort was in possession
of the earldom, specially requiring the obtainment of a
charter. It was one truly characteristic of the period, and
which exemplified the value of such documents to the
burgesses. It may therefore be briefly narrated:—In the
previous chapter it has been stated that the first of the earls
Robert allowed the burgesses to settle their disputes in
relation to their burgages by submitting them to the decision of the Portmanmote, instead of by fighting a duel—to
re-institute, in fact, their ancient local court, instead of
continuing the barbarous custom of ordeal by battle; the
burgesses paying in acknowledgment of the permission to
do this a certain tax upon every gabled dwelling in the
High Street, called the gable-penny or gavel-penny. Now,
the son and successor of the earl (Robert le Bossu) remitted

the payment of this impost, and for ever quitted his claim thereto, by a charter. This document was placed, with the other archives of the town, in the hands of Lambert, the clerk, who was their proper custodian. Being considered in that day a rich man, the burglars of the locality were tempted to break by night into his house, to which they also set fire; the charter in question, with other writings, being consumed in the conflagration. After the death of Le Bossu, another clerk, Simon the Accursed *(Simon Maudit)*—the affix to whose name suggests a legend of popular malediction and odium—had in farm the bailiwick of Leicester, and in the gratification of an extortionate nature, demanded payment of the gavel-pennies, knowing that the townsmen had no legal evidence to produce of their remission by the earl recently deceased, now that the charter was destroyed. When they claimed to be excused from the tax, he challenged them to produce their warrant of quit-claim, and he insisted on their paying the tax, and succeeded, in short, in his unjust demand, defying all their attempts to escape from the payment. The successors of Maudit also persisted in the extortion until the year 1254, and the burgesses actually submitted to it for sixty-four years. In that year, however, an inquisition was made in presence of the town bailiff, the mayor, and other jurors, when the circumstances were proved in evidence, as well as those relating to the way in which the tax called "bridge-silver" had originated; and the consequence was the concession of a charter by Simon de Montfort, wherein he abandoned all further claim to the gavel-pennies and the bridge-silver—not, however, without receiving an equivalent from the burgesses in the surrender to him of certain rents paid in the town and out of the South Fields.

A third charter given to the townsmen by Simon de Montfort was nearly a transcript of that conceded by

Robert Fitzparnel, and copied in the preceding chapter,* in which the former earl relinquished the enforcement of the pence which had been collected from the people on account of their exemption from servile labours, and for other reasons therein assigned.

The age in which Simon de Montfort lived was one of superstitious prejudice and commercial ignorance, when the Jews were held in detestation, equally because of their religious tenets and their position as money-lenders. In Leicester, as everywhere else, despised, persecuted, and cruelly used, they lived apart from the Christians in an obscure quarter by themselves. Among the ruins of the Roman town, which had been left to fall to pieces by the slow process of time, was one huge pile which modern archæology (as already said) has identified with the western gateway. In the arches of this structure the outcasts sought shelter, and hence in succeeding ages it has been known as the "Jewry Wall." But even this miserable retreat the townsmen begrudged to the Israelites, and they therefore besought the earl's consent to the banishment of the ancient people of God from the walls of Leicester. In consequence he granted this charter:—

"Simon de Montfort, son of earl Simon de Montfort, lord
"of Leicester, to all who may see and hear the present
"page, health in the Lord ! Know all of you that I,
"for the good of my soul, and the souls of my ances-
"tors and successors, have granted, and by this my
"present charter have confirmed, on behalf of me and
"my heirs for ever, to my burgesses of Leicester and
"their heirs, that no Jew or Jewess in my time, or in
"the time of any of my heirs to the end of the world,
"shall inhabit or remain, or obtain a residence, in
"Leicester. I also will and command, that my heirs

* See page 46.

"after me observe and warrant for ever that liberty, "entire and inviolate, to the aforesaid burgesses. In "testimony of this I have confirmed the present charter "with my seal. Witnesses: Sir Aumery of Mittun, "Sir Walter de Aquila, Sir Roger Blund, chaplain, "William Bassett, William of Miravall, and others."

A usage, called the law of Borough English, had long prevailed in Leicester, in accordance with which the youngest son succeeded to the property of his father. It was alleged that owing to a defect of heirs and their weakness, the town was falling into ruin and dishonour, and therefore a change in the established custom was necessary. The burgesses accordingly supplicated the earl to grant them a charter, under the authority of which their eldest-born sons might succeed to the paternal inheritance and habitation—to what has been already legally designated "the burgage." The earl listened to the prayer, and granted the charter requested, which was dated at Westminster, in the month of October, 1255.

From the grants of Simon de Montfort, the extent of his power over the townsmen is to be inferred. With his consent the pasturage rights could be exercised; by his authority burdens could be imposed, such as gavel-pennies and bridge silver; by his fiat Jews and Jewesses could be expelled from the borough; and with his sole sanction the laws of inheritance could be changed. So that within the walls of Leicester he was a petty sovereign.

Allusion has been made to the various officers of the Guild, but not to its place of meeting. In their hall the fraternity often assembled. There the Aldermen sat of old to instal new members, the Council to discuss the common affairs, and the brethren to elect their officers. An ancient building had been used as a Guild Hall prior to the year 1254; but another was then purchased. It was conveyed

by William Ordriz to Peter Fitz-Roger, the Mayor, and the
"Commune" of Leicester; as the Guild is called in the
ancient conveyance. Within its walls the whole fraternity
appear to have had festive days, when they caroused over
ale and wine, with which they ate bread alone; and as the
fines were often paid in tuns of beer, and sometimes in
casks of wine, these occasions were not infrequent.

By the annual accounts of the Guild (of which the earliest in existence may be dated in the year 1257) it is
demonstrated that the body known by that name raised
and expended the public finances. In the items entered
on the back of the skins on which the names of new members are enrolled, it may be perceived that the charges for
the bread and wine consumed at the meetings, the "fines"
due to the king from Leicester, the cost of repairs to the
gates and walls of the town, the outlay upon the bridges,
the presents made to the Judges, and, in fact, all other
public obligations, were defrayed out of the Guild purse.
Most of the entries directly name the objects of the payments. They are as follows:

"To Robert Griffyn for the cost of the refreshment pro-
"vided at the morwenspeches, 12d."

"To our lord, the king, for the common fines due to him
"from Leicester, 20 marks."

"For repairs done to the four gates and walls of Leicester,
"£4 19s. 4d."

"For the bridges of Leicester, 42s. 11d."

"For sixty-one sextaries and one flagon of wine, sent to
"the Justices by the community of Leicester, and for
"a cask of wine bought for the Justices, £6 12s. 4d."

"To the bakers for bread, £4 19s. 3d."

"For one new purse, bought for the community of the
"Guild, 6d.

"For a new seal, made for the Guild, 4s. 6d."

In the reign of Henry the Third, the fairs of Stamford and Boston were the resort of the merchants of Leicester. There they took their coarse cloth, their wool, and the skins of sheep and cattle. To them were allotted rows in which to exhibit their goods and commodities, and all the regulations affecting the placing, the sale, and the genuineness of these were made by the Guild, whose members alone were allowed to visit the fairs for commercial purposes. The principle of all these arrangements was restrictive, because it was considered that the Guild brethren should reap advantages corresponding to the contributions they made to the purse of the community.

CHAPTER VI.

BOROUGH OF LEICESTER (CONTINUED).

Simon de Montfort's fall at the battle of Evesham in 1265, was followed by the usual consequences of treason. His family was deprived of the honours and possessions he had enjoyed, and the earldom of Leicester was then at the disposal of the monarch, who conferred it upon his second son, commonly called Edmund Crouchback. It is noticeable that this earl granted no charters to the burgesses of Leicester. The presumption is that the grants already repeatedly made by his predecessors had established the rights of the inhabitants beyond the necessity of confirmation, and therefore they were henceforth taken for granted. The only evidences the municipal archives present of the connection between him and them are afforded in the entries relating to money advanced to him by various townsmen, a large portion of which was expended in paying the wages of carpenters, smiths, and masons employed at Kenilworth Castle, where Earl Edmund was then residing; besides various amounts paid for provisions supplied to his crossbowmen and archers, and for articles for his own personal use.

It is not improbable that during the Barons' Wars, which occurred before and shortly after the middle of this century, the administration of town affairs had become loose and irregular, the unsettled state of the country having produced everywhere a relaxation of the usual proceedings of the local courts and their officers. Long delays occurred in the hearing and determination of causes by the Portmanmote of Leicester, and its powers had been lessened, so that suitors failed to obtain justice. Under these circumstances, the Earl, with his Council, and with the assent of the Mayor and Jurats, and all the commons of the town, made certain amendments in the regulations of the Portmanmote, which bore date 1277. The particulars aid in showing that its jurisdiction was in essence and effect the same as that of the earlier and simpler institution, the Court Leet, though probably more extended, in consequence of its adaptation to the greater requirements of an increased population.

The old mode of doing justice was, it appears, slow—half a year, or a whole year, sometimes intervening between the making of a complaint and the appearance of the defendant, who, keeping himself out of the way, and concealing his goods in chambers, evaded appearance. To remedy this injustice it was provided that the defendant should be summoned to the Portmote at its earliest court "by witness of the neighbour"—that is, by proclamation made, or information given to the surrounding neighbourhood, and, after that, if the defendant did not appear, a simple distraint was made upon him; after which, if he still made default, he was obliged to find sureties for his appearance. It seems there were two kinds of distress, the simple and the great distress; the issue of obstinate recusancy in appearing being the levying of considerable fines both upon himself and his sureties.

By the next regulation, the defendant's sureties were to be apprehended if they did not compel him to appear in court to answer for himself; and it was provided, that, whereas before the date of the changes here described a debtor might, in answer to a plaint, say "have-law," and thus postpone a case indefinitely, without finding sureties, this dilatory plea should in future only avail for the postponement of a cause until the next court, and that if the defendant should have recourse to this plea, he was bound to find sureties, or leave his property in pledge for his punctual appearance at the succeeding court.

It had occasionally happened that a trader would fraudulently remove his goods out of the borough to avoid payment of the demands upon him, and his pledges would also escape comparatively "scot free," by a payment of expenses or a shilling to the bailiff; this evil was met by falling upon the pledges, by distraint, until they produced the debtor.

The earl's tenants *in capite* could sue first in this court, and afterwards in the earl's court, which led to great trouble and delay. This was to be remedied by providing that if a suitor desired to appeal to the earl's court he must do so " within the third court."

The next regulation provides a remedy for an irregular usage, in reference to the old custom of a defendant having recourse to the wager of law in an action for debt. The defendant was in the habit of interrupting the plaintiff by exclaiming from time to time "Thwertnay"—he did not owe the debt—to the discomfiture of plaintiffs who were not acquainted with the practice, and occasionally to their unjust defeat in cases in which the wager of law was not applicable. This was put an end to by regulations which secured the plaintiff an uninterrupted hearing, and prescribed the mode in which the defendant should answer.

The succeeding passages in the document of which these paragraphs form an abridgment, relate to the compulsory expulsion from the town of Leicester of persons who were "bold to make bates, batteries, and hamsockens" (which last word means the assaulting of men in their own houses —a very serious offence in the estimation of our ancestors); to the appointment of attorneys to conduct legal business in the borough court; the abatement of suits in case the plaintiff made default; the abrogation of a rule against the institution of cross-suits, under which rule it often happened that if a man had beaten another the sufferer was prevented suing his adversary for damages, by the institution of a suit against him by the wrong-doer; to the abrogation of a regulation by which courts were not to be held whilst the merchants were "at the great fairs of the land"; to the abolition of the custom of distraining "neighbour for neighbour"; to providing a remedy for those who, on the occasion of a sudden emergency, either of a public or private kind (as, for example, the arrival of any distinguished person in the town) borrowed money, bread, or wine of their neighbours, and did not repay within forty days; to the fair assessment of public levies, so that the great were to no longer favoured, whilst the poor were compelled to pay; and finally, to enabling the lord's bailiff to break down walls, or to pierce pales, in order to effect a distress for rent or service.

The inhabitants of the Bishop's Fee, being tenants of the Bishop of Lincoln, lived under his manorial jurisdiction. Being also amenable to such taxes as he was empowered to levy upon them, in the language of the time they were required to "scot" in the Fee of the Bishop. While, however, occupying this relationship to him, and doing suit and service to him, and owning the authority of his court— the same in character and objects as the Court Leet of the town—the bishop's tenants had the opportunity of entering the Merchant Guild, of enjoying the advantages it afforded, and of sharing the privileges its members had obtained for themselves in the charters conceded to them by the earls of Leicester. But owing to their peculiar position and suburban residence, attempts were made by some of them to secure the benefits without discharging the obligations of the guild brethren, and disputes in consequence happened between the two parties. These rose to a height which needed the special notice of the Earl of Leicester and the Bishop of Lincoln, and therefore the case was laid before

Sir Walter of Helyon and Sir John of Metingham, the Justices of the King, and "other good men;" an agreement being the result, which embodied the terms on which the bishop's men acquiesced in living with the guild and the townspeople.

It was covenanted that when the tenants of the bishop were desirous of entering the Guild Merchant, they should be received into it according to the forms and usages accustomed, and should be allowed to enjoy all the franchises and free customs belonging to the guild, within and without the town, and in all things. And that the tenants of the bishop should henceforth be in "scot" and "lot" in all those things which to the guild belonged, or the burgesses, according to their taxation. And at all times when the burgesses made gifts or presents to the king or the queen, on their coming into the "parts of Leicester," to the amount of twenty pounds or less; and to their lords of the town of Leicester, at their coming, to the value of twenty marks or less; and to the ministers of the king, and to others, on account of aids, and for maintenance of the franchises of the guild,—the tenants of the bishop should pay scot and aid to the gifts and presents, according to the portion which to them belonged, by reasonable taxation made by honest men, for him, and them, and upon the one and the others; so that if the gift and the presents should be made, by common accord of the tenants, of greater value than before mentioned, then the tenants should pay scot to it according to the agreement made. And if gifts or presents should be made of greater value, without the will and consent of the tenants, they should not be held accountable to contribute. And when the town of Leicester escheated unto the mercy of the king, or paid fines for trespass which touched the community of the guild, the tenants of the bishop should pay scot to it in the form aforesaid; but it was not in the least to be understood for mercy nor for fines paid for the trespass of any particular person, who ought to be punished for his trespass; unless by the common agreement of the tenants. Neither was it to be understood that the tenants should pay scot in like manner for amerciaments which touched the community of the town and not the community of the guild; except those who had lands or tenements in the town of Leicester, who were burgesses of the town. And when the officers of the king should come to assay the weights and measures in the town and suburbs, and they should take fines of the one or the other, by reason of trespass found in the weights and measures, the tenants of the bishop should take care to pay scot to such fine according to the portion which belonged to them. And in order that all these contributions should be assessed lawfully, so that every one might be charged for the portion which to him belonged, they might choose and call together honest men, tenants of the bishop, to see and hear the account which belonged to them, in like manner with the honest men of Leicester, and the aforesaid burgesses and the commonalty of Leicester. And the tenants of the bishop should take care, for them and their heirs and assigns and their successors, that they thenceforth should hold, keep, and do, and in all points use, all the things aforesaid at all times. In testimony of all these things the respective parties interested attached their seals to the agreement. (1281 A.D.)

In this way the men of the Bishop's Fee became associated in local and municipal affairs with the townsmen; though owing allegiance to different lords.

A few years after the date of this agreement, an ordinance was adopted by the guild affecting the position of the sons of the deceased brethren. It indicates a care for them, on the part of the fraternity, which may either be assumed to evince special consideration for the welfare of the young burgess, or taking precaution as to his means of fulfilling the obligations he might incur as a guild member. The ordinance was to this effect:

The Mayor and Jurors, at a meeting in the Hall of the Guild, held on the Friday before the Feast of St. Peter in Cathedrâ (Jan. 18), in the twenty-first year of the reign of king Edward, the son of king Henry, considered that every heir, after the decease of his father, should have all the liberties which his father had had, as well in the suburb as in the town, without any payment for the enjoyment of them; and that he should have the following vessels—better lead in the furnace, a better brass jar, better basin and ewer, a better mazer, a silver spoon, and a better table with a better table-cloth. And if his father died indebted to any one, and, over and above the aforesaid goods, there were not chattels sufficient to pay his debts, then those things were to be sold until all his debts were fully discharged.*

It is obvious most of the articles above named were those which the young burgess needed in his humble household—the lead in the furnace being the only exception; and it seems probable the guild required he should be

* Consideratum fuit in aula Gilde die veneris proximo ante festum Sancti Petri in Cathedra per Thomam Gounfrey tunc maiorem Leycestriæ Laurenciam le Sellor, Robertum de Wylughby, Ricardum sub muro, Willielmum Baudewene, Robertum de Dalby, Henricum de Loseby, Johannem de Burton, Johannem Martyn, Thomam le Ryder, Walteram de Welham, Willielmum le Palmer, Willielmum le Engleys, Johannem de Knytecote, Willielmum de Threngeston, Radulphum de Honecote, Ricardum Geryn, Radulphum de Hodynges, Willielmum de Bracina et Johannem Gagge, Juratos ejusdem, quod quivis heres post decessum patris sui natus in villa Leycestriæ habeat omnes libertates quas pater suus habuit tam suburbio quam infra villam sine aliqua redemptione, et quod ipso habebit vasa postdicta, scilicet, melius plumbum in fornace, meliorem ollam eneam, meliorem pelvim cum lavatorio, meliorem mazerium, cochlear argenteum, mensam meliorem cum meliore mappa. Et si pater suus indebitatus fuit versus aliquem et bona sua non sufficiant preter bona predicta, illa bona vendantur donec debita sua pences omnes plenarie fuerint soluta. Ista consideracio fuit facta die veneris predicto anno regno regis Edwardi filii regis Henrici vicesimo primo.—*Borough Charters, Laws of Portmanmote*, &c., pages 37, 38, & 39.

provided with them, in order that he might have a sufficient number of movables on which the local and other taxation might be levied. Even those, however, were not to be his until his father's debts had been paid by a sale of the household stock of the deceased guild brother.

Edmund Crouchback, Earl of Lancaster and Leicester, died in the year 1299, and was succeeded in the latter title by his eldest son, Thomas. By this time, the relationship of the burgesses to their feudal superior had undergone a considerable modification, when compared with what it was a century previous. It was now productive of oppressive taxation rather than of tyrannical interference with the daily conduct of the townsmen. The records of the period attest that heavy imposts were levied upon the burgesses for the benefit of the barons of the House of Plantagenet, which were openly resisted in the public places. But this was not all; when Thomas, Earl of Leicester, involved himself in the quarrel between his kinsman, Edward the Second and the insurgent barons, it was from the purses of the townsmen of Leicester that a considerable portion of the requisite funds was taken, and it was by the services of many of them in the field that the Earl's cause was maintained. Thus far, then, their vassalage was still evidenced. In January 1322 the Earl directed a letter to the seneschal of his castle at Leicester, commanding him immediately to choose some of the most powerful men of the town of Leicester to meet him at Tutbury. The recruits disliked the service imposed on them, and refused to proceed from Tutbury to Pomfret in pursuance of the orders of the Earl's Lieutenant; and but for a threatening letter sent by the Earl to the Mayor and community of the town, would have deserted from his standard.* A month or two afterwards, the King's lieutenant visited the place with a

* History of Leicester (1849), pages 103 and 104.

commission to raise men on the King's behalf, when the Mayor and principal townsmen agreed to raise a contingent of fifty soldiers from the borough, besides forwarding a fine of two hundred pounds to their royal master. In this way (as the reader will have observed) the people of Leicester were subject to the extortionate demands of their King on the one side, and their Lord on the other. About the 16th of March, the Earl was defeated near Boroughbridge, and shortly afterwards executed near his own castle at Pomfret.

Still, in spite of the foregoing drawbacks upon their municipal privileges, the inhabitants had extensive control over their own internal arrangements. The Mayor, the Bailiff, and the "good people of Leicester" (as a contemporary document records), were empowered to keep the peace within their walls; they forbad men from going through their streets in coats of mail, to the injury of the public peace; they fixed the prices of bread, wine, and beer; they prohibited forestalling and nuisances; and they regulated other local matters.*

Another arrangement, which increased the authority of the burgesses over their own town affairs, was a grant made by Henry Duke of Lancaster and Earl of Leicester, the brother of the last unfortunate local potentate of that family. It will be better understood after a preliminary explanation of the nature of the dues owing by the townsmen to their feudal superior. As their manorial lord, he had the appointment of the bailiff of the town, suburbs, and fields of Leicester, to whom a variety of fees were paid by virtue of his office, in connexion with executions, and so forth. The Earl was also entitled to the profits arising out of the Portmanmote, the fairs, the markets, and all the local courts. The goods forfeited by fugitives and felons

* *Ibid*, 105.

were his property. The keeping of prisoners in the town was also part of the Earl's authority. When the inhabitants required timber for the reparation of their shops, houses, and shambles, they were under the necessity of taking it in the woods of the honour of Leicester, from time to time, on such terms as the Master Forester chose to dictate. Through the mixed, and sometimes contending jurisdiction of the Earl's bailiff and other officers, with the servants of the municipal authorities, much annoyance and vexation, accompanied by exactions, were undoubtedly occasioned, and the townsmen were doubtless made to feel their dependence upon the agents of the Castle.

In the year 1376, they found a remedy for the evils they experienced, by purchasing with a payment of twenty pounds yearly, the appointment of the bailiff, the annual profits of the courts, and the other advantages hitherto accruing to the Earl in the way already specified. By this grant, the whole town was emancipated from the galling intervention of functionaries selected by the Earl, and placed over them in a position offensive to their love of personal and municipal independence.

In the period intervening between the death of the last of their Norman lords, and the accession of the third of the Plantagenet family, the townsmen had reaped all the benefits of material prosperity, which appears to have made steady progress under the protection afforded by their Merchant Guild and their charters. This was indicated, among other things, by the payment of annual salaries to public officers. In the first instance, the Mayor does not appear to have had a settled salary, nor a sergeant, nor a clerk; but towards the close of the thirteenth century, mention is made of an annual present to the Mayor of a mark (for salmon), of an allowance of half a mark to the Town Sergeant, and of a similar sum to the Clerk, who kept the rolls and the accounts of the borough. In the thirty-fourth year of Edward the Third's reign, the Mayor was allowed forty shillings for his feast, and forty shillings for his clerk's table.

The mention of the Mayor's feast, it may be explained, arises from the usage which had some time before gradually come into existence in this manner: When the Mayor had been chosen at an annual meeting of the Guild, it was customary for him to proceed, some short time after, to the Castle, where the Earl's steward was holding his court, and there to take an oath of allegiance to his feudal lord, in presence of the deputy of the latter. At the conclusion of the ceremony, the Earl's steward was invited to an entertainment given by the Mayor, the costs of which were defrayed in the manner suggested by the item already named.

In the thirty-ninth year of Edward the Third, an additional sum of ten shillings and sixpence yearly was paid to the Mayor, and in the fiftieth year of the same king's reign the sum of six pounds was paid to the Mayor, to cover the expenses of the annual feast, and the stipends of the clerk and sergeant. In the reign of Richard the Second (October 1379), certain ordinances were made in the Guildhall of the town, by the Mayor and Jurors, and with the unanimous consent of the whole community, placing the Mayor in a still higher position, and appointing and defining the duties of the Town Chamberlains.* Under these regulations the Mayor was discharged from all accountability for the public moneys in future, and an annual allowance of ten pounds of silver was made to him by the community. Of this sum, forty shillings was for his feast, and if he did not hold the feast he was not to receive the amount; forty shillings for the wages of his sergeant, and if he had not

---

* History of Leicester, page 135.

one he was not to receive that sum; and twenty shillings for the wages of his clerk, who was also to attend upon the Chamberlains for the time being, and if no clerk were appointed the Mayor was not to receive the amount mentioned. The remainder of the ten pounds, the Mayor was entitled to for his other charges and expenses. It was ordered that if any costs should be incurred on account of presents made to the king, the lord of the town, or any other lord or lady whatsoever, in the name of the town, the expenses were to be incurred with the consent of the Mayor and Jurors, and twenty four of the commons, or by the whole of the community. The chamberlains (who were paid fifty shillings each annually for their services) were authorized to keep in proper repair the gates, walls, ditches, pavements, and houses of the town, at the cost of the whole community, and to collect all rents, and other payments belonging to the Merchant Guild and the community. They were further required to render reasonable and faithful account of their stewardship, at the end of each year, before the mayor for the time being, and certain auditors specially elected.

These changes in the salaries and functions of officers—particularly the chamberlains—were not made theoretically, but followed the acquisition of property by the community. Before the middle of the fourteenth century, its property consisted only of a tenement, a chamber, and a small place yielding a few pence annually. The remainder of its yearly income was derived from special taxation, fees paid on entrance into the Merchant Guild, and the tolls collected at the bridges. Early in the reign of Richard the Second, however, the income of the body was augmented by rents derived from an estate, acquired by the town in an adjoining village, which was subsequently increased by further additions. In this way the appointment of chamberlains became an absolute necessity.

The last resident Earl of Leicester was John of Gaunt (who died in 1399), whose son, Henry the Fourth, inherited the title and manorial rights and privileges of the line from which he was descended. But thereafter the townsmen were left uncontrolled by the presence of the officials of the castle; and it will be inferred, after the close of the fourteenth century, reached an atmosphere of comparative freedom. For some generations, greater security to person and property had been enjoyed, riches had been accumulated by frugal and industrious burgesses, and the pressure of feudal influences had been removed. Under the monarchs of the House of Lancaster—the descendants of their ancient earls—the inhabitants possessed all the advantages already enumerated, and for more than a century they had elected representatives to serve them in parliament; they therefore now occupied a position second to few, and equal to that of the general body, of the English boroughs.

In the middle of the century, the war began between the Houses of York and Lancaster, which continued for thirty years. In this furious contest, the towns played a conspicuous part, and at the battle of Towton Moor, in particular, the troops they sent to the field aided in determining the fortunes of that memorable day. Owing to the excesses committed by the followers of the Red Rose in their marches southwards of the Trent, in the campaigns occurring previous to that action—and their threats of occupying the "south country," and taking all they desired, and doing what they pleased with the wives and daughters of the people of that region—the Southerns were roused to a high pitch of fury, and a stern determination to vanquish their enemy or die themselves in the attempt. The various forces of each borough were led to the field under distinctive banners, on which were emblazoned well-known crests or heraldic emblems. The Harrow of Canterbury, the White

Ship of Bristol, the Black Ram of Coventry, the Leopard of Salisbury, the Wolf of Worcester, the Dragon of Gloucester, the George of Nottingham, the Boar's Head of Windsor, the Wild Rat of Northampton, and lastly the Griffin of Leicester, were unfurled on the side of the Yorkist leader on that terrible day on which between thirty and forty thousand men were slain; and the consequence of which was the establishment of Edward, earl of March, on the throne, as Edward the Fourth of England.

The successful monarch was not unmindful of the services rendered him on this eventful day, as a circumstance occurring in the following year attests. In the month of May, 1462, when he was visiting his Castle of Leicester, Robert Rawlett, the Mayor, and Thomas Green and John Roberts, the two parliamentary representatives of the borough, were admitted to an interview with him, and he then granted to the inhabitants a gift of twenty marks yearly, for twenty years, in requital of the aid they had given him against his enemies. About the same time, also, he conferred upon them by charter the power of appointing yearly four magistrates, to whom was entrusted very extensive jurisdiction, which ensured exemption from the intervention of the justices resident in the county.

Eight years after, the king (who had returned as a fugitive from the Continent) was again supported by the townsmen of Leicester, who, under Lord Hastings, accompanied him to the fields of Barnet and Tewkesbury, in the latter of which Edward was once more completely triumphant. He rewarded the town a second time, by making to it a grant of twenty pounds yearly for twenty years, and giving it a license to hold a fair in May, in all time succeeding.

It is in these plain facts of history the reader will perceive the mode in which the boroughs profited by the struggles of contending dynasties. The story which is told of Leicester might doubtless be also told of the contemporary communities which contributed their levies to the victorious hosts of Edward, and needs no rhetorical flourish to impart to it significance and interest. It is the simple and unvarnished fact which the buried annals of many an ancient town would disclose, could they be disentombed.

CHAPTER VII.

BOROUGH OF LEICESTER (CONCLUDED).

It will have been noticed by the reader that a portion of the community has been referred to which was not a constituent part of the Merchant Guild. This body is sometimes called the "Commons," or the "whole community" of the town. The individuals of whom it was composed, not being enrolled in the Guild, were incapable of carrying on trades in the borough, and ineligible to fill any of the municipal offices; but they were liable to the local taxation, and to be called on to fill the less honourable civic posts, involving services of an onerous nature: they were the persons who were called upon, in the customary phraseology, to "pay their scot" and "bear their lot," as unprivileged inhabitants. In the troublous period of civil war, this class appears to have forced itself into prominence, and to have claimed a share in the public business. In the archives of Leicester, it is stated that on the election of the Mayor, and at other Common Halls, they would enter into the Guild Hall and there remain during the progress of the proceedings. The record says that the Mayor and his Brethren had been informed by writing and otherwise, that the king (Edward the Fourth), and certain of his lords, had knowledge of "divers ungodly rules and demeanings, especially among the Commons of the town, aforetime used at their Common Halls; and for those, take such displeasure that, without a remedy found, it is likely to turn to the perpetual prejudice and foredoing of the large liberties and franchises of this town (the which God defend?) and not only that, but such great rumours and speech runneth to divers parts of this realm, the which soundeth and likely is to grow to the great rebuke and dishonour of all the body

of this town and every member thereof." A "remedy" was
found for this evil (as it was then regarded) at a Common
Hall held in the year 1467, by the assent and agreement
of the Mayor and his Brethren, and all the Commons there
being present; which consisted in the adoption of a law or
ordinance, enacting that if any person or persons entered
and remained within the Guild Hall, at any Common Hall
therein held, unless they were "franchised,"—that is to
say, entered into the Chapman's Guild—then such offender
or offenders were, by the command of the Mayor, to be
committed to prison, there to continue forty days on the
Mayor's grace, until he or they paid eleven pence to the
Town Chamberlains for the benefit of the town; or otherwise to remain incarcerated for the whole period. As it is
also intimated that some of the inhabitants would cry out
or name aloud one of the Mayor's Brethren to the office of
the Mayoralty, thus anticipating the orderly nomination of
the chief magistrate and the usual formalities of the occasion, it was decided that any person violating the rule
should be fined six-and-eightpence, and be liable to impri-
sonment in addition.

In this condition the town government continued until
the reign of Richard the Third; the freedom of the populace having apparently degenerated into licentiousness; for
in the first year of that monarch's reign—probably on the
occasion of his visit to the Castle in the month of August
—an ordinance was agreed upon to divide the town
into twelve wards, over each of which an Alderman was
appointed to preside. The reasons assigned for this measure were the generally-prevalent rumours concerning the
existence of evil-disposed persons, vagabonds, petty bribers,
rioters, and bad women, and the evidences of neglect in the
state of the public roads and buildings, which occasioned
great annoyance to the king's people, and "foreboded the
utter destruction of this great town."

The movement for the expulsion of the Commons from the assemblies of the ruling body of the place was revived in twenty-two years after the date of the last effort at municipal exclusiveness. In this instance, the interference of the king (Henry the Seventh) had been invoked by the high burgesses against the mass of the unprivileged inhabitants. The feeling which had slumbered for a generation awoke to work, with greater effect than before, in opposition to the troublesome commonalty. The event which brought the struggle to a final issue was the receipt of a mandate from the monarch, addressed to the local authorities, which ran as follows:—

"Henry, by the grace of God King of England and of
"France, Lord of Ireland. To our trusty and well-
"beloved the Mayor, Bailiffs, Comburgesses and Bur-
"gesses of our town of Leicester, parcel of our Duchy
"of Lancaster, and to every of them, greeting:

"And forasmuch as we have been informed, that at
"every election of the Mayor there, or Burgess of the
"Parliament, or at any assessing of any lawful impo-
"sition, the Commonalty of our said town, as well poor
"as rich, have always assembled at your Town Hall—
"whereas such persons as be of little substance or rea-
"son, and not contributors, or else full little, to the
"charges sustained in such behalf, have had great
"interest, through their exclamations and headiness,
"to the subversion, not only of the good feeling of our
"said town, but likely to the often breach of the peace
"and other inconveniences, increasing and causing the
"fall and misery and decline of our said town, and the
"great discouragement of you the governors thereof;
"for reformation whereof, and to the intent that good
"rule and substantial order may be had and enter-
"tained there, from henceforth we will and straightly

"charge you, and also command you, the said Mayor,
"Bailiffs, and twenty-four of our Comburgesses of
"our said town, now being, and that for the time that
"shall be, that at all Common Halls and assemblies
"hereafter to be holden there, as well for the election
"of the Mayor, of the Justices of the Peace, and Bur-
"gesses of our Parliament, as also at assessing any
"lawful imposition or otherwise, ye jointly choose and
"call unto you our Bailiff of our said town for the
"time being, and only forty-eight of the most wise and
"sad Commoners, inhabitants there, after your discre-
"tion, of the same commonalty, and no more; and you
"then to order and direct all matters occurrent, or
"happening amongst you, as by your reason and con-
"science shall be thought lawful and most expedient.
"Given at our Palace of Westminster, under our seal of
"the said Duchy, the second day of July, the fourth
"year of our reign."

Six weeks after the receipt of this precept, the Mayor and his Brethren made it known to the townspeople. They then held a meeting, at which they took an oath on the Evangelists that they thereafter, in obedience to the mandate, would not take upon themselves the offices they held, on the election of the commonalty, but only under the appointment of the Mayor, his Brethren, and the Forty Eight of the commonalty who had been selected from the entire number. The penalty for a violation of this agreement was to be expulsion from the magisterial bench and the council.

Shortly after, the election of the Mayor occurred. The retiring Mayor (Thomas Davy), his Brethren, and the Forty Eight, chose a townsman named Roger Tryg to be Chief Magistrate; but the commonalty, unwilling to part with their ancient rights without a struggle, nominated another inhabitant, named Thomas Towithby, who had already held the offices of justice of the peace, auditor of the accounts, and steward of the fairs. This procedure was, in its way, bold and formidable—so formidable, in fact, that it brought down a direct and special mandate from the king, to set it aside. It is to be remarked, however, that while Henry annulled the choice of the commonalty, he did not confirm that of the new oligarchy; for, instead, he re-appointed Davy, the retiring Mayor—in this act showing that he felt it inexpedient to take upon himself, by his own arbitrary authority, to sanction the organic change which had been made in the constitution of the municipal body. It is further noticeable that the nomination of Tryg was made under the sanction of a precept under the seal of the Duchy of Lancaster; this act implying that it was as the representative of their ancient feudal lords, not as monarch, that the king extended his hand to interfere in the affair.

The consciousness, on the part of the sovereign, that his mere mandate was insufficient to warrant the revolution proposed to be effected, was evidenced by the passing of an act by both Houses, in the year following, which embodied the changes in the municipal constitution specified in the precept, thus rendering them legal. Another royal warrant (Nov. 6, 1490) directed the payment of the sum of £7 above the usual fee to Davy, the Mayor. Towithby, the champion of the commonalty, had already paid the penalty of his endeavour to resist the tide of royal and magisterial tyranny; for two months before, the Mayor and Justices had resolved that he should be "utterly excluded" from the Bench "for evermore."

From this time forth, therefore, the "Commonalty" were deprived of the right they had immemorially possessed of taking part in the election of parliamentary representatives and municipal officers; and the power in those respects was thereafter monopolized by the Mayor, his Brethren, and the Forty-Eight.

In the same reign, the power centred in the hands of the Local Justices was largely increased. Henry the Seventh confirmed the charter of Edward the Fourth (in the year 1505) on this subject,* enabling the municipal body to select Magistrates independent of those acting for the county, and imparting to them authority to adjudicate in cases of murder, felony, and other crimes, as well as in cases of counterfeiting, clipping, washing, and falsifying money, hitherto not possessed by them. The right of the inhabitants to be taxed separately from the county was also granted to them—the Mayor and certain Burgesses to be the assessors of the local burdens. At this date, therefore, the Recorder and Four Justices formed a tribunal, invested with the highest functions: to them, sitting on the Bench in the Guild Hall, was it competent to order a fellow-townsman to the gallows: elected by an irresponsible body, they were the arbiters of life and death, of ignominy and innocence: the most solemn issues were then under the control of a class over whom the remainder of the townsmen had ceased to have influence.

For nearly a century the current of local affairs ran uninterruptedly; as, however earnestly the excluded portion of the townspeople might have wished to resist the act which disfranchised them, and might have desired to overthrow the new system, they found themselves utterly powerless to do so. In consequence, the régime introduced by the Tudor dynasty remained in undisputed force and unchecked operation. The great changes ensuing upon the Reformation, however, very materially extended the importance of the acts of the Municipal Assembly; for the town then acquired a considerable property which had belonged

* History of Leicester (1849) page 206.

to ecclesiastical bodies and suppressed guilds and chantries. Hitherto its power of acting in a corporate capacity, in the sale and purchase of houses and land, and in the power of suing and the possibility of being sued, had been limited, if not altogether wanting. Legally, it had had no entity in these respects; and accordingly its action was impeded by the inability to move regularly and independently as a municipality. It was therefore a matter of political necessity that it should be endowed with corporate functions. Under these circumstances, the inhabitants obtained a CHARTER OF INCORPORATION from Queen Elizabeth, by virtue of which the Mayor, his Brethren, and the FORTY-EIGHT, were designated "the Mayor and Burgesses of the town of Leicester;" were enabled to buy and sell lands by that name; were authorized to sue and be sued by that name; and were guaranteed all the privileges, rights, jurisdictions, and so forth, which they had previously enjoyed. By the same grant, the authorities received in fee farm, for a yearly rent, payable to the Crown, the lands and houses formerly belonging to four religious guilds in Leicester, a lease in reversion of a considerable estate, and other properties.

From this time the municipal body ceased to be known as the "Merchant Guild," and was ordinarily called the Incorporation, or by the abbreviated form of the term, the CORPORATION; while all those persons who were admitted to share in its privileges, and were allowed to be eligible to fill its offices, were no longer known as "Brethren of the Guild," but as "Freemen." The ancient records testify, that the phraseology was at first mixed, in relation to the appellation given to the principal inhabitants; but, ultimately, the old terms fell into disuse, and no relic of the old institution was left in the language of the people, except in the name given to the place of Municipal Assembly, which was always called the "Guild Hall."

A second charter was bestowed on Leicester by Queen Elizabeth (1590) which embodied in a collected form the municipal rights of the inhabitants, and the civil and criminal authority vested in their rulers. Instead of the Portmanmote, the charter confirmed the right of the Mayor, Recorder, Bailiffs, and Stewards, or one of them, to hold a court on every Monday, weekly, there to adjudicate in actions of trespass, debts, accounts, and similar cases; and it also confirmed the right of the Mayor and Justices to try criminal offences, murder and felony excepted.* With increased wealth, the members of the Corporation began to assume the insignia of greater official importance, and to affect a pomp and pageantry not before so fully witnessed. Accordingly, they were authorized to elect five Sergeants-at-Mace, whose duty it was not merely to act as lesser bailiffs, but to carry maces of gold and silver before the Mayor in procession.

Under the sway of the Tudors, Local Government had tended irresistibly to a system of self-election and irresponsibility; under the Stuarts, it reached its point of culmination. We have seen that until the reign of Edward the Fourth the commonalty had a share in the election of the Municipal officers and the Parliamentary representatives, and that then they were formally excluded altogether from the Common Halls. After that date, it seems,† the official body and the people each elected a member separately. This was the first encroachment upon the popular principle; and the system continued in force until the year 1554, when the members of the Local Government assumed the right, independently of the commonalty, to select the two Burgesses in Parliament. Thirty

* The power over life and death, given by Henry the Seventh's charter, was thus withdrawn.

† See History of Leicester, pp. 199, 200.

years after, the Corporation elected their members at the dictation of the Chancellor of the Duchy of Lancaster and the Earl of Huntingdon, a nobleman of the locality. But even this course left the town an appearance, at least, of free choice. Only one step further in political degradation was possible—the absolute surrender of the right of election at the command of the sovereign. This took place on the receipt of a writ from the Queen's Privy Council (dated from Windsor Castle, Sept. 19, 1586), requiring the Corporation to re-elect the retiring members, in a style which rendered refusal virtually impossible. The usage remained unbroken of selecting candidates, directly or indirectly subject to Court influences, until the establishment of the Commonwealth, during which period the municipal body was mainly composed of Parliamentarians. At the restoration (1661) the commonalty re-asserted their ancient claim to interfere in the election of representatives; the "Freemen" and "Commoners" then voting for the candidates, and those whom they selected being permitted to retain their seats by the decision of the House of Commons.

The devices of the Tudor sovereign for depriving the body of townsmen alike of their local and Parliamentary franchises, were even surpassed, in cool contempt of human rights, by the two last of the Stuarts; as will be seen by the attempts they made to deprive this town of even the shadow and semblance of local government with which Henry the Seventh had left it municipally pauperised. The circumstances were these : In October, 1684, the Earl of Huntingdon forwarded letters to the town, suggesting the surrender of its charter to Charles the Second. The Chief Magistrate and his colleagues consented to the measure at a Common Hall, and forwarded a petition to the king, praying that their liberties and privileges might be re-granted, accompanied with such restrictions as his Majesty might consider necessary. The Earl of Huntingdon then made private inquiries into the characters of the members of the Corporation, with the intention of omitting from the new charter the names of all who were opposed to the Court policy. In December the new charter was passed, and showed what was the design, in reference to local freedom, of Charles and his Ministers; for while it professed to guarantee to the Mayor and Corporation the possession of all their ancient rights and privileges, it required that the election of *all the officers and members should be subject to the king's approval, and that they should be liable to removal whenever he might think proper!* In addition to which, the only portion of the Corporation which might be liable to be influenced by public opinion—the Common Council—was reduced in number from 48 to 36.

The same course as that pursued here was carried out all over England; but at Nottingham the townspeople had the spirit to resist the procedure, and some of them were in consequence convicted in the King's Bench of having created a riot. The object of the monarch was, to be enabled to pack juries for judicial purposes, and to influence the election of members. Even the historian Hume—the apologist of the Stuarts—thus remarks upon their unparalleled acts of despotic authority: "It seems strange that the independent Royalists, who never meant to make the Crown absolute, should be yet so elated with the victory obtained over their adversaries as to approve of a precedent which left no national liberties in security, but enabled the king, under like pretences, and by means of like instruments, to recal anew all those charters which he was at present pleased to grant; and every friend to liberty must allow that the nation, whose constitution was thus broken in the shock of faction, had a right, by every prudent expedient, to recover that security, of which it was so unhappily bereaved."

The last of the Stuarts completed the climax of folly in the closing year of his inglorious reign, by displacing a large number of the Aldermen and Common Councilmen in the various boroughs. They were of the Church party; and Dissenters were put in their places. His motive in this proceeding was to gain the support of the Nonconformists, while opposing the Church, with a view to facilitate his plans for the ultimate establishment of Roman Catholicism as the State religion. But the insincere and hollow project failed: the falseness of the monarch was perceived by all parties; and he became a fugitive, dying an exile from the country whose liberties and religion he had sought to overthrow.

In the first year of the reign of William the Third, the charter was restored to Leicester, and from that time remained in force—the fruitful source of a variety of abuses (as now universally admitted)—until the act was passed under which the present form of municipal government was initiated. And then, neither to king, nor to baron, nor to abbot, did the burgesses of English towns owe the regaining of rights and privileges which had existed during the Saxon Heptarchy, and even during the Middle Ages; but to the joint action and deliberation of the three estates of the realm. Taking their rise under the easy rule of the Saxon monarchs, surviving the Norman invasion, sustaining the shock of medieval vicissitudes, and submitting to overthrow by the despots of the Tudor and Stuart dynasties, the local independence and responsible government of the townspeople once more came into being under the House of Hanover, in the reign of the Fourth William; since which date they have flourished with unabated vigour and usefulness.

CHAPTER VIII

THE BOROUGH OF PRESTON.

In the case of St. Alban's, we have seen how a town grew up to the position of a municipality under the walls of an abbey, and without deriving (as far as history teaches us) any advantage from the Roman institutions which were once in operation in a city previously occupying the same or an adjacent site. In the case of Leicester we have traced the development of a borough occupying the very ground formerly tenanted by the Romans, and subsequently dependent on feudal barons of Norman origin and lordly scions of the House of Plantagenet. In approaching the case of Preston, we meet with no traditions of Roman rule nor associations of long-continued baronial connection with the place. Its early history is involved in complete obscurity. The name, however, indicates the origin of the place as a town belonging to priests—the Priest, or (as the word was more anciently pronounced) the Prest Town, being its distinctive appellation from the first, preceded by no Roman antecedents whatever. Before the year 700, we learn there was a church erected on the site—one of those primitive structures of wood, constructed in the rudest fashion. Standing on a high bank, whose base was washed by the tides and waves of the broad but shallow Ribble, it offered advantages in commerce and navigation which probably led to the selection of the spot, at a date when the ancient Roman stations higher up the stream had become deserted, through the changes in its bed and banks. It is on record that in the year 700 Wilfrid, archbishop of York, repaired the church; from which we infer that the fabric and land around it were then, and had probably been originally, in the possession of the monks of the ancient northern metropolis. In the year

927 the church was formally dedicated to Wilfrid, who had been canonized in the intervening period. The district of Amounderness (including Preston) passed from the hands of the ecclesiastics of York to those of Tosti, the Duke of Northumberland, one of the sons of Godwin, and the brother of king Harold.

At the Norman Conquest, the Saxon proprietors were dispossessed of their domain, the district being allotted to Roger of Poitou, one of the companions of the Conqueror. Subsequently rebelling against his royal master, he was attainted and his lands were forfeited; but Rufus, the son and successor of William, restored to the Poitevin his estate on the banks of the Ribble. When the Domesday Survey was taken there were only three churches in the district, and one of these was at Preston. Ultimately, Roger of Poitou was banished the kingdom, and Henry, the Conqueror's fourth son, gave the towns and villages of Amounderness to his nephew, Stephen, afterwards king of England. On his decease, his son, William, earl of Mortmain and Boulogne, received the lands from Henry II., by agreement. While this monarch was the manorial lord, he gave the burgesses a charter, in which he "confirmed" them in the possession of their local rights and privileges—the expression of the document indicating their pre-existence; and we are justified by the analogy supplied in the case of Leicester, in assuming that they had not been introduced subsequent to the Conquest, but may safely conjecture that they had been enjoyed by the burgesses in the time of Wilfrid; probably from the very outset—seeing that the only way successfully to found a new community of traders was to guarantee to them a measure of local self-government and the right of uniting in a Guild for their mutual and collective benefit. This, if the early ecclesiastics of York were the founders, was all the more likely; as they could retain only a feeble hold directly over a population living in a quarter so remote from their place of residence.

The Charter of Henry II. was in these terms, the Latin of the original being translated into modern English*:

"Henry, &c., King of England, &c., to his archbishops, "bishops, abbots, earls, barons, justices, sheriffs, and "all his officers and liege men throughout England, "greeting. Know ye that I have granted, and by this "my present charter have confirmed, to my burgesses "of Preston, all the same liberties and free customs "which I have given to my burgesses of Newcastle-"under-Lyne. Wherefore, I will, and firmly command, "that my aforesaid burgesses of Preston have and "hold, well and in peace, freely and quietly, fully and "entirely, and honourably, both within the borough "and without the borough, all those liberties and free "customs (saving my right of administering justice) "which the burgesses of Newcastle-under-Lyne have, "as I have granted, and by my charter confirmed, to "them the aforesaid burgesses of Newcastle.—Wit-"nesses: G. of Ely, and I. of Norwich, bishops; God-"frey de Lucie, earl; William de Maundeville, Ranulf "de Glanville, Hugh de Cressy, Ralph Fitzstephen, "Bertram de Verdun, Hugh de Laci—Given at Win-"chester."

The reference to the charter of Newcastle-under-Lyne† renders its production necessary, in order to the illustration of the position occupied by the burgesses of Preston under Henry's charter. It was as follows:—

" Know ye that we have given, and by this our present " charter have confirmed, for us and our heirs, that our

* *A History of Preston Guild*, by William Dobson and John Harland F.S.A., page 7. 1862. London Simpkin, Marshall, & Co.

† *Ibid*, page 6.

"town of New Castle under Lyne be a free borough, and that the burgesses of that borough have a Guild Merchant in the said borough, with all liberties and free customs to such Guild Merchant in any wise belonging; and that they may pass through all our dominions, with their merchandize, buying, selling, and trafficking, well and in peace, freely, quietly, and honourably; and that they be quiet [or quit] from toll, passage, pontage, stallage, lastage, ulnage, and all other customs. Wherefore, we will, and strictly command, for us and our heirs, that the free burgesses of the said town receive all manner of security of peace, soc and sac, toll, infangthief, utfangthief, hang-wyte, home-soken, gryth-bryce, plyt-wyte, flyt-wyte, ford-wyte, fore-stall, child-wyte, wapentake, lastage, stallage, shoowynde [shewing or scavage toll] hundred, averpenny; and for all treasons, murders, felonies, riots, the chattels of all felons, and all other customs and actions throughout our realm, and the Marches of Wales, and our dominions as well in England as in any other of our territories.—Given under the hand of the Reverend Father R. Bishop of Chichester, our Chancellor, at Fakenham, the 18th day of September, in the 19th year of our reign."

The reader who bears in mind what has been already states in regard to the constituent rights and privileges of a "borough," will see that Newcastle-under-Lyne and Preston were merely "confirmed" by Henry II. in all that has been described as necessary to place them in that category. They were made "free boroughs;" they were exempted from the jurisdiction of the hundred or division in which they were situate, and rendered independent of external or neighbouring authority, having thus an individuality of their own. They had their Guild Merchant—their association of inhabitants combined to manage their purely municipal affairs. They were protected in their mercantile enterprizes when travelling beyond their own town, and were entitled to exemption from the customs imposed in the towns they visited. They had "soc" and "sac," "infangthief," "outfangthief," already explained, and so forth—in brief, they had civil and criminal jurisdiction, and the power to levy and appropriate to the public use fines for offences, and certain customs charged upon strangers who frequented their fairs and markets.

What were the fines the burgesses could impose, appears from the catalogue of names recited in the charter. They could levy fines upon persons for house-breaking; for breaking the peace; for quarrelling; for avoiding military service; and for buying wares privately before being brought to the public market. If a bondwoman were pregnant without her owner's consent, a fine was levied upon her and recoverable.*

The burgesses could compel non-resident tradesmen, who attended their markets, to pay a duty on wares sold according to the quantity; to pay a duty for setting up a stall; to pay for merely exhibiting their wares. They could also levy a small tax on the dwellers in the borough, on the same principle as that enforced upon a hundred or division of the county, and another, to defray the cost of the king's carriages on his journeys; and they could require a periodical production of weapons by the townsmen. The only respect in which the inhabitants of Preston differed from those of Newcastle-under-Lyne was, apparently, that while the latter had the right of administering justice, the former had not—the exception probably extending only to the higher class of offences.

* These fines were called Homesoken, Grith-breach, Flytwyte, Fordwyte, Forestall, and Childwyte.

The enquirer into municipal history is materially assisted in the case of Preston by a manuscript still extant, in which the usages relating alike to the general management of the town, and its civil and criminal affairs, are codified. This document, called the Custumal,* is assigned to the thirteenth century, and was therefore compiled within three or four generations after the date of Henry the Second's Charter. It enables us to ascertain yet more clearly than the charter, what was the internal condition of the borough at the early period under notice, which will be found in all main points to accord with the picture presented by its contemporary town, Leicester.

The privileged inhabitants were the "burgesses." To qualify a man to become a burgess, he was obliged to possess a plot of ground, called a "burgage," having a frontage of twelve feet, and to go into the town court and give to the Reeve or Alderman 12d., taking his burgage from the Bailiffs, and paying one penny to their servant to certify that he had been made a burgess in court. A born bondman from the adjoining district, by dwelling anywhere in the town, and holding a burgage, and being in the Guild, and paying scot and lot for a year and a day, could emancipate himself from his lord, and thus acquire municipal freedom.

When thus franchised, the burgess acquired privileges and incurred responsibilities, pertinent to his novel position. He shared with his fellows in the corporate authority and jurisdiction belonging to the borough—and he enjoyed exemption from local imposts in all places beyond his own town, and from any intermeddling by the sheriff of the county, in any pleas, plaints, or disputes. While a born bondman could not give his daughter or granddaughter in marriage without the permission of his lord, the burgess

* *A History of Preston Guild*, p.p., 73 to 78.

could do as he pleased in this respect without consulting any other person, or paying any tax to any person. The widow of a deceased burgess might marry whomsoever she pleased; unlike the bondsman's widow, who could not marry without the feudal lord's consent. When a burgess died a sudden death, his widow or heirs might succeed to the undisputed possession of his land and chattels—the bondsman's widow having no such right, the feudal lord being entitled to step in and claim everything as his property. The burgess had right of common pasture everywhere, except in corn-fields, meadows, and inclosures; and none but burgesses, members of the Guild Merchant, were allowed to make any merchandize—that is, to carry on business—in the borough, unless with the special sanction of the body of burgesses.

As they had privileges, they encountered corresponding responsibilities. These were—to pay taxes, to serve in municipal offices, and to serve in war, if need was, under the banner of their lord—or, to express it in the words already frequently used, they were bound to pay their "scot" and bear their "lot." The taxes were of two kinds—local and general. Of the first, we learn little in the Custumal; but as expenses were incurred on behalf of the community, regularly and sometimes extraordinarily, the townsmen were liable to be called on to contribute to them according to their individual means. Thus, there is the following clause:

"Also, if burgesses, by the Common Council of their "neighbours, shall travel for any business of the town, "their expenses shall be rendered to them when they "return."

It is probable the ordinary payments made on entrance to the Guild, and periodically required, met the local demands upon the body; and therefore any specific levies

—other than those imposed on foreign merchants visiting the markets and fairs—were not necessary. The general taxation consisted of this—at the date of the Custumal, the townsmen held under fee-farm of the king; instead of paying the various taxes in detail due to the king as lord of the manor, they gave him an equivalent in full, undertaking the collection of them among themselves, by the agency of their own bailiff. The arrangement is thus alluded to in the Custumal :

"The Pretor of the Court shall collect the king's farm at "the four terms of the year, and shall go once for the "farm, and another time if he pleases, and shall take "away the door of such burgage, and the burgess shall "not replace his door until he have paid his debt, "unless at the will of the Pretor."

That, in addition to tax-paying, the burgess was occasionally called on to serve as a soldier, is evident from a clause in the Custumal which declares that "the aforesaid burgesses shall not go in any expedition unless with the lord himself, unless they may be able to return on the same day." It was further enacted,

"That if he shall be summoned when the justice of the "town shall be in the expedition, and shall not go, "and shall acknowledge himself to have heard, he "shall give amends 12d.; if he denies to have heard "the edict, he shall clear himself by his own oath; "but if he shall have essoin [excuse for non-appear-"ance]—to wit, either by siege, or his wife's lying in "childbed, or other reasonable essoin, he shall not "pay. If he is going with the person of our lord the "the king, he cannot have essoin."

We have to collect from mere incidental reference in the Custumal what were the public offices. The words "Prefect" and "Pretors" are used when the principal functionaries are spoken of in the Latin original; and we infer from the allusions made to them, that the former was the Mayor, and that the latter term meant the Bailiffs. The Mayor was also still known in the middle of the thirteenth century as the Reeve or Portreeve—the Norman word "Mayor" not having as yet extended to this town. The Mayor and Bailiffs had their servants in attendance upon them. The duties of the Mayor consisted chiefly in presiding over the Guild and the Court of Portmote. His person was protected by the imposition of a fine of indefinite amount on any person who might strike him in Court, and by a fine of 40s. upon any burgess who might strike him out of Court. The duties of the Bailiffs were confined chiefly to the collection of the tolls, dues, and taxes in the borough; but they held all unoccupied burgages in their hands, and probably the enforcement of fines and punishments was part of their authority.

The Guild is thus alluded to in the Custumal:

"These are the liberties of Preston in Aumundrenesse:
"So that they have a Guild Mercatory, with Hanse,
"and other customs and liberties belonging to such
"Guild; and so that no one who is not of that Guild
"shall make any merchandize in that town, unless
"with the will of the burgesses."

The burgesses were thus, obviously, all guildsmen, and guildsmen and burgesses were synonymous terms; seeing that the burgesses exercised the power of giving to persons not members of the Guild permission to carry on business in their town. What the "Hanse" meant, as distinct from the Guild, it is impossible to say; as the term is usually employed as identical with Guild. Probably it was inserted in the Custumal to prevent misconception in relation to the full meaning of the words "Guild Mercatory." The Guild, then, meant the totality of the burgesses in their purely municipal position; the "customs" and "liberties" pertaining to it being at the time so generally and thoroughly known as to render further description superfluous. The insertion of the clause respecting the Guild, in the very outset of the document, shows that it was the chief institution of the place; inseparable from its existence; without the existence of which it would have had neither freedom nor independence; and, in fact, the tangible embodiment and corporate realization of the community.

Equally evident is it that the jurisdiction of the Portmote Court was distinct from that of the Guild. Its functions were, as repeated before, confined to civil and criminal matters. The burgesses of the Guild were all amenable to its authority, and compelled to attend certain of its sittings. The Custumal is explicit on this head:

"Also, a burgess shall be bound to come to no more than "three portmotes yearly, unless he shall have plea "against him, and unless he shall come to one great "portmote he shall be amerced 12d."

Of the identity of this institution all along with the Court Leet, no reasonable doubt seems to remain: in the clause just given it is indicated that pleas were regularly decided by it. In another clause, it is prescribed that in case of the right to a burgage being disputed, the respondent be called on to prove possession, for a year and a day, "in Court by the oath of two of his neighbours." In another clause, it is stated that the amerciament "in our Court" shall not exceed 12d. In another clause, the process for the recovery of debts is provided to take place before "the Court."

The custom of deciding disputes by duelling was in existence in Preston at the date of the Custumal; though abolished earlier in other boroughs. Supposing the date of the document to be 1250, the duel would have been appealed to in Preston after having been abolished for more than a century in Leicester.* The case in which it came into use was when the burgesses of the Portmote Court decided on its necessity. It is referred to in the Custumal in this way :—

"Also, if a burgess shall sell for more than the assize,
"he shall be amerced 12d.; and he who bought in
"nothing; the burgesses of the court aforesaid shall
"have duel, or fire and water to make judgment."

The meaning of this is, that if a townsman sold any article—as bread or beer, for example—for more than the usual price fixed by the authorities, he should be fined 12d.; the buyer not being fined. It does not seem that the second clause of the sentence is necessarily connected with the first; but that it was inserted rather accidentally or inadvertently than otherwise, since it has no connection with the one preceding. It is a mere statement of the fact of the burgesses of the Portmote Court having the alternative of submitting all disputes, concerning which the testimony on both sides was conflicting and which they could not satisfactorily decide, to the ordeal of battle between the litigants, or to the ordeal of exposure to fire or to water, either hot or cold; the former being the Norman course of proceeding, the latter the Saxon—and both being based on the belief that a direct Divine interposition in favour of the innocent or adverse to the guilty would ensue. In another clause of the Custumal, the duel is mentioned; the ordinary fine of 12d. leviable by the Court being raised to 40s., in the instance in which a defendant demanded a duel and the combat took place; the inference being that the burgesses of the Court, disapproving of the duel, and perhaps knowing that it might be and was generally

* See page 39.

appealed to by the stronger against the weaker burgesses, imposed a heavy payment by way of obstacle to the exercise of brutal strength by a dishonest townsman against a neighbour unequal to him in physical capacity. A third allusion to the duel occurs in another paragraph of the Custumal. After enacting that no burgess should be taken into custody either by the lord of the town or the Manor, if he had found sufficient securities for his appearance when called on, it proceeds:—

"So of claim made of a burgess by any knight, whosoever the knight may be; if a duel be adjudged between the burgess and the knight, the knight may not change [in other words, find a proxy], unless it be found that he ought not to fight" [that is, was personally unable].

In the trial by combat, the knight and the burgess were therefore placed on an equality; unless, perhaps, the former was entitled to fight on horseback, while the latter was on foot; which would be an unequal contest.

In regard to punishments, other than by payments of money, little is said in the Custumal. In one case—wherein a burgess broke the regulations respecting the sale of bread and ale—a fourth offence was punishable by a very heavy fine, or, as a last resort, by his being placed in the cuck-stool. Even when one burgess wounded another by stabbing him, the offender and the offended might amicably arrange, on the former paying 4d. for every hidden cut and 8d. for every visible wound. The extreme penalty of the law seems to have been inflicted by the royal officers.

At some period subsequently to the granting of the charter by Henry the Second, the burgesses of Preston established a custom peculiar to their borough, of revising the rules and regulations under which their affairs were managed. This custom was observed once in twenty years,

its designation handed down to modern times being Preston
Guild. The first of these interesting observances of which
any record has been preserved took place in the month of
June, 1328. It seems to have been primarily held for the
purpose of amending old regulations and instituting new
ones, and secondly as an occasion of local festivity and
enjoyment, associated with the picturesque processions and
impressive ceremonies of the Church, so much in accordance with medieval tastes—the whole being supposed to be
under the tutelary protection of the Saint of the locality.

By reference to the text of the account of the "Guild"
of 1328, we learn that the celebration had been held
at a date some time previous; if twenty years before (as
was not unlikely to be the case), the first Guild which we
have any historic authority for believing to have taken
place, would occur in 1308; the orders made at that time
being recapitulated in the document just mentioned. The
substance of them may be thus conveyed:— The first
requires that all inhabitants who have not obtained their
freedom through the Guild Merchant be fined by the
Mayor and twelve of the commonalty whose names were
already enrolled in the Guild Merchant—thus proving distinctly that it was indispensable to becoming a burgess to
be a member of the Guild Merchant. The second order
empowers the Mayor to discharge of his freedom for ever, any
man actively opposing, or not actively aiding, the borough
authorities in the keeping of the peace. The third order
shows that the bailiffs had to keep the accounts and to
collect the taxes imposed by the Guild; to render their
accounts on a certain day, and to have forty days' grace for
getting in arrears; after which they were to be imprisoned till they had collected and paid all. The fourth
order prohibits ex-mayors and ex-bailiffs from interfering
with the twenty-four jurors (who were doubtless the Town

Council of the day) in the election of the mayor, under a penalty of twenty shillings or loss of freedom ; but the ex-mayors and ex-bailiffs were entitled to sit upon the bench with the mayor as aldermen. The fifth order considerately provided that decayed burgesses, unable to pay their yearly contributions, should not lose their freedom because of poverty. The concluding orders were not of such a nature as to need any explanation.

When the Guild Merchant held its appointed ceremony in 1328, it adopted certain ordinances which it may be well here to epitomise. It will have been noticed that the name given to these periodical assemblages was "the Guild," that term standing for what in modern times would be called "the twentieth anniversary meeting of the Guild Merchant,"—the name of the institution itself being given to its periodical meeting. In the account of the Guild of 1328 it is simply called "a mayor-court;" and is represented to have been held before Aubrey Fitz Robert, the Mayor, and the bailiffs of the same town, "on Monday next after the feast of John the Baptist, the year of the reign of king Edward the Third after the conquest of England, the Second." Of these ordinances, the first declares that the Guild Merchant shall be amenable to the regulations about to be explained. The second orders that it shall be lawful to the said Mayor, Bailiffs, and Burgesses, their heirs and successors, to hold a Guild meeting every twenty years, or earlier if they had need, to confirm the charters affecting their franchise or jurisdiction. The third ordinance enacted that all corporate fees during the Guild year should be applied to the purposes of the Guild celebration. The fourth ordinance insisted upon every son of a burgess purchasing his freedom in the Mayor-court, and not in any other court—in other words, recognizing no other burgess-ship except that obtained by becoming a member of the

Guild Merchant. The fifth ordinance is so decisive in its meaning, that we insert it entire:

"Also the same mayor, bailiffs, and burgesses, with all "the commonalty have ordained, by a whole assent "and consent, that all manner of burgesses, the which "is made burgesses by court-roll and out of the Guild "Merchant, shall never be mayor, nor bailiff, nor ser-"geant, but only the burgesses whose names were in "the previous Guild Merchant; for the king gives the "freedom to the burgesses who are in the Guild, and "to none others."

The meaning of the last ordinance seems to be that, although some among the inhabitants had acquired a spurious kind of burgess-right by the entry of their names upon the manorial court-rolls, they were not allowed to take any active part in municipal affairs. It would appear, from the proceedings of this occasion, that not even a shadow of a doubt remains, that what in modern times is designated "being a freeman" was anciently the same thing as being a member of the Guild Merchant; that what in modern times is called the Corporation was anciently called the Guild Merchant; and that our modern municipal system is merely the development, with alterations and modifications, of the old Guild Merchant.

Although it was resolved to hold "a Guild" every twenty years, no repetition of the affair seems to have taken place until near the close of the fourteenth century; or at least no record is extant relative to any such meeting. Sixty-nine years after, however, the Guild was again observed with the customary formalities. The disturbed state of the country in the north of England, owing to the frequent incursions of the Scots, is supposed to have interfered with the orderly progress of events in the borough of Preston; so it was not until the year 1397 that the usage was revived. The record designates it "the Guild Merchant of the town of Preston-in-Amounderness." The names of those whose fathers were not in the Guild, and who therefore made a payment on entrance, finding two securities each, are given ; with the names of those who with their fathers were in the fraternity. The articles or statutes adopted by the Guild were five in number. From the first, of these it appears twelve burgesses were associated with the mayor in the government of the town, instead of twenty-four, as at the Guild preceding, and that they could deprive a burgess of his freedom—that is, expel him from the Guild Merchant—for any infraction of the liberties of Preston. The second article requires that before a burgess can be elected mayor, he shall have first filled the office of bailiff. By the third, refusal to serve a fitting office was visited by a withdrawal of freedom. The fourth and fifth related to the bailiffs' accounts.

It is to be concluded that the fundamental principles of the Guild had been too long established, and were too well known, to require any re-statement on this or subsequent occasions. Accordingly when, in the year 1415, a Guild was held (eighteen years after that of 1397) the articles made on the last occasion were merely confirmed and ratified. On comparison with the records of previous Guilds, we are informed,[*] the repetition of the same surnames shows the succession of offices in a few wealthy and influential families of those remote days.

Another Guild was held in the year 1439, when the names of a mayor, two bailiffs, and twelve aldermen, are recorded as those of the officials of the time. Other Guilds were held in 1459, 1500, and 1542, of which records have been preserved. In regard to the last named, it may suffice to state that a lengthy recital of the Guild arrangements of

[*] *History of Preston Guild.*

the time accompanies the record of it in an ancient manuscript, giving rise to these observations in the book to which we are indebted for much of this summary of the history of Preston Guild* :—" It is impossible to read these old Guild laws without seeing in them a strenuous assertion of their sole right to confer freedom, or the franchise upon any one : for, even though inherited, freedom was not regarded as complete, until due suit and service, oaths and fees, had been rendered to the Guild. Again, the mayor's authority and that of his council is maintained with the greatest vigour, and those who resist it are rebels ; those who betray the municipal confidence, or expose the poverty of the town, are false and forsworn traitors, not merely to be degraded in social position by losing their freedom, but their toll is to be taken of them daily, as of persons not to be trusted or credited beyond the passing day."

For the same reasons which rendered formal incorporation necessary in English boroughs generally, Preston was incorporated in the year 1566, by the charter of Queen Elizabeth. In that document the Queen grants to the mayor, bailiffs, and burgesses power to plead and be impleaded as a corporate body, and the right to have a common seal : also that there should be twenty-four of the more discreet and worthy men of the borough to assist the mayor and bailiffs, and be called "the principal burgesses," forming a common council, and having power with the mayor to enact ordinances for the better rule and government of the borough. Accompanying these concessions is the recognition of the old Guild Merchant, with all the liberties and free customs appertaining to such a Guild, as they have heretofore enjoyed. The old Court of Portmote was continued as a three weeks' court. A view of Frankpledge of all the inhabitants and residents is also included

* Messrs. Dobson and Harland's *History of Preston Guild*.

in the charter, which does not appear to have imparted any new liberty or privilege to the inhabitants, but merely to have enumerated the contents of all previous charters, and given a general confirmation of their contents to the inhabitants. The only new feature it presents is the incorporation of the borough; after which date the municipal authorities were no longer known by the name of the Merchant Guild, but as the Corporation, and the brethren of the Guild were thereafter recognized as the "freemen of the borough."

The Corporation hereafter was in fact the Merchant Guild, but under another name and modified in character. The "Guild" continued to meet every twenty years, after the year 1562; but it was, in truth, a mere municipal carnival, associated with sumptuous banqueting and popular pageantry. The streets, on the recurrence of these festivals, witnessed long processions of the neighbouring nobility and gentry, the mayor and other local officials, and the trade companies, preceded by banners, and enlivened by the minstrels, who delighted each successive generation.

Meanwhile, the Stuarts confirmed the system of self-election originated by Elizabeth in her charter; Charles the Second having rendered the municipal system still narrower, in consonance with his endeavour to obtain in his hands autocratic authority, controlling alike the municipal and representative systems. In this state the local government of Preston remained until the passing of the Municipal Reform Act, when it underwent the transformation which English Corporations generally experienced.

Every twenty years, however, down to the year 1862 has the phantom of Preston Guild been summoned from its sepulchre, dressed out in the costume of the modern age; its grotesque presentment only enkindling a smile among the lovers of mere utility, or a vague sentiment of interest in the ancient institution. But it should not be forgotten that the pageant of our age reminds the municipal enquirer of the value of an institution which, in the reigns of our Henries and our Edwards, was identified with the individual freedom of the burgesses and the independence of the borough, when the mass of the people of the surrounding districts were in a state of abject serfdom and wretched dependance.

CHAPTER IX.

THE CITY OF NORWICH.

In the extreme east of this island, during the time of its occupation by the Romans, a station known to them as *Venta Icenorum* was in existence, resembling those to which allusion has been made in previous pages. As its name suggests, it was a town of the Iceni—a powerful tribe of ancient Britons, who had stoutly resisted their Italian invaders. A few miles north of the station, the shallow waters of an estuary of the German ocean rolled; when the Venta of the Iceni was probably a populous place; but in the course of a few centuries they gradually retreated, finding in one part a channel by means of which they made their escape to the sea, and leaving exposed an elevated promontory.

Two consequences followed these changes of nature. One was, that the Roman city ceased to be approachable by ships, owing to the river which passed by it becoming filled up with mud and weeds; and the other was, the erection upon the promontory of a rude fortification, round which houses in due time clustered, on the island-summits left bare, glad to obtain the protection thus offered. The Roman city accordingly sank into insignificance, and the newer site gained the importance lost by its deserted neighbour, at some date between the middle of the fifth and before the close of the seventh century. The settlers in the latter locality were doubtless of Saxon origin, who, to distinguish their place of abode from the older town, simply designated it, in their language, the North-vic, or North-town, afterwards pronounced Norwich. An ancient rhyme not inaptly tells the story of the transition of fortune from the Roman place (subsequently known as Caistor) to its rival and supplanter:

> Caistor was a city when Norwich was none,
> And Norwich was built of Caistor stone.

Caistor dwindled away into a village, and Norwich became populous. Its castle, defended by a deep ditch, sheltered the houses from the assaults to which they must have been liable, by their proximity to the shores on which, generation after generation, troops of Scandinavian adventurers landed in quest of plunder and in hope of conquest. Alfred the Great and his successors had a Mint in Norwich, its establishment indicating that the place had become, towards the close of the ninth century, a seat of regal authority and a centre of traffic. This also tempted the cupidity and the rapacity of the Danes, who under their king Sweyn sailed with their whole fleet up to Norwich, which they captured and destroyed; finding no difficulty probably in the latter proceeding, as the buildings would be only frail fabrics of wood, which, on the application of the torch, would speedily fall beneath the spreading flames. The place lay in ashes for a few years only; as Sweyn returned to it, and reconstructed the town and castle. During the sway of Edward the Confessor (1041–1063 A.D.) the number of inhabitants largely increased, there being then a population of 1320 burgesses; in fact, excepting London and York, there was not a more populous city in England.

In the Domesday Survey, the entries point to the probability of the same state of relative position of the inhabitants to the king having existed here, in the reign of the Confessor, as at Leicester and elsewhere. We have seen that the usage was to pay to the monarch certain customs, and to enjoy local independence in return for the payment; the date of this arrangement, though mentioned as recognized in the time of the Conqueror, being by inference long anterior thereto. The Norwich burgesses paid twenty pounds to the king and ten pounds to the earl, besides twenty shillings in the shape of aids, six sextaries of honey, and a bear with six dogs to bait him. When these tributes were paid to the royal officers, the citizens were left free to manage their own local affairs. But there were also other local lords by whom they were ruled; for while 1238 of them were amenable to the jurisdiction of the king and the earl, fifty others lived within the soke of Stigand, and thirty-two were settled upon the land of Earl Harold, afterwards king, and were under his authority. But the sheriff had no power of interference within the city, as it constituted a hundred by itself. The burgesses owed suit and service only to their respective lords, in their Courts Leet.

When the Normans under their duke, William the Bastard, extended their marches to Norfolk, they found the citizens of Norwich, the descendants of the Saxons and Danes, prepared to offer a formidable resistance. A large proportion of the houses were destroyed in the siege, and large numbers of the inhabitants killed. Still when, twenty years after, the return was made of the number of burgesses in the place, it was found to be 1565, who were paying public customs, while there were 480 cottagers, in addition, whose poverty obtained for them an exoneration from the payment of local taxes. The crown dues were augmented; for the inhabitants now paid seventy pounds' weight of silver to the king, one hundred shillings as a free gift to the queen, with an ambling palfrey, twenty pounds of uncoined silver to the earl, and twenty shillings as a free gift to Godfric. The population having so considerably multiplied, a new borough was added to the old one, containing the pleasantest part of the locality; where thirty-six French burgesses (as the Normans were then called) and six English burgesses, had their abodes.

The strenuous opposition offered to the Conqueror by the citizens seems to have rendered strong measures necessary for their subjection; the government of the city being vested in Roger Bigod the earl who, seated in the Castle, had supreme control over the inhabitants. Under him, the sheriff collected the royal dues, two-thirds of which were paid over to the king's treasury, and one-third to the earl. At this time, the Castle ruled the city in all things, and the local self-government in civil and criminal affairs, and in matters purely municipal, which had been in operation previous to the Conquest, it may be presumed, was now suspended. The citizens were also compelled to serve as soldiers, when occasion required, and were consequently involved in all the ill fortune which might attend the Norman baron who forced them to do military duty. How painfully and disastrously this system operated, the following event will show :—

In the year 1074, Ralph de Gaël, a Breton lord who had accompanied the Conqueror, was earl of Norfolk. Having contracted marriage with Emma, the sister of Roger, earl of Hereford, he had fixed the performance of the ceremony to take place in Norwich, to be followed by a banquet at the Castle, although the king had sent a message from Normandy to forbid the union. At the latter were present Norman bishops and barons, Saxons friendly to the Normans, and Welchmen; and among the guests was Waltheof, earl of Huntingdon. The repast was sumptuous and the wine circulated freely, so that the tongues of the company were unloosed. The bride's brother loudly and haughtily blamed the king for refusing his consent to the marriage, and the Saxons vehemently applauded the invectives. Speech after speech full of angry complaint and menacing defiance ensued, and the meeting ended in a conspiracy; Waltheof yielding to the persuasions of the leaders to join them in their resolve to dethrone William, and set up a new government. The malcontent earls collected their forces, and threatened a formidable insurrection; but the principal body of them, under the earl of Norfolk, were defeated in a battle at Fagadun, and the same fate attended the followers of the earl of Hereford in the west, the earl himself being captured. The citizens were very unfortunate. Having under the command of the newly-married countess resisted the king's troops, the royal vengeance fell upon them in the shape of multiplied vexations, which forced many of them to flee to Beccles, and Halesworth in Suffolk. They were pursued to those localities by Roger Bigod, Richard de St. Clair, and William Noyers, and their persons seized, and they were reduced, being already in a condition of irredeemable beggary, to a state of complete serfdom. When these events had terminated, scarcely five hundred and sixty burgesses remained in Norwich.

Circumstances like these were well calculated to prolong the withholding of civil and municipal privileges from the citizens. Under the king's provost, residing in the Castle, they knew nothing of local freedom. Their persons and their property were alike at the mercy of Roger Bigod, who, on the decease of William [1087, A.D.] held the castle for Robert Curthose, duke of Normandy, the Conqueror's eldest son, and subsequently for William Rufus, the fourth son, who succeeded his father, and lastly for Henry I. But in the reign of this monarch, when Hugh Bigod had succeeded his father and brother in the earldom, the hope of freedom dawned upon the citizens; for the Conqueror's youngest son kept his Christmas at Norwich, in the year 1112, and was so gratified with the reception he met with that he granted them a charter, embodying the same privileges and liberties as the city of London then enjoyed.

At this time, the disparity in size of London and Norwich and other towns was only slight, compared with what it became in following centuries. It thus happened that the same sort of municipal regulations which the Londoners found suitable for their requirements were considered desirable by the men of Norwich, and had, in all probability, been asked for by them in an interview with the king, while enjoying the festivities of the winter season in the Castle adjoining their city. The clauses of the charter granted by Henry I. to the inhabitants of the metroplis render us acquainted with its internal state in relation to municipal administration, and with the arrangements which were conceded to the people of Norwich. Omitting the mention of details in the London charter, which applied exclusively to that city, and premising that the sheriffwick of London and Middlesex was let to the citizens of London for three hundred pounds, the articles were these :[*]

"That the citizens of London shall appoint as Sheriff such one from among themselves as they shall think proper.

"Also, that the said citizens shall appoint such person as Justiciar from among themselves as they shall think proper, to keep the Pleas of the Crown, and to hold such Pleas; and that no other person shall be Justiciar over the said men of London.

"Also, that the citizens of London shall not plead without the walls of the City in any plea.

"Also, that the citizens of London shall be quit of Scot and Lot, Danegeld and murder; and that no one of them shall wage battle.

"Also, if any of the citizens shall be impleaded in pleas of the City of London, such man shall deraign himself by such oath as shall be adjudged in the City.

"Also, that no one shall be harboured within the walls of the City; and that no lodging shall be delivered

---

[*] See the "*Liber Albus* of the City of London, translated by Henry Thomas Riley, M.A. London: 1862."

"to any one by force, either of the household of his
"lordship the king, or of any other household.
"Also, that all men of London shall be quit and free,
"and all their goods throughout all England and the
"sea-ports, of toll, passage, lastage, and all other
"customs.
"Also, that the Churches and Barons, and citizens may
"have and hold quietly and in peace their sokes, with
"all their customs.
"Also, that no man of London shall be amerced in a sum
"of money beyond his were, namely, one hundred shil-
"lings; in pleas, that is to say, which pertain unto
"money.
"Also, that there shall no longer be miskenning in the
"Hustings, or in the Folk mote, or in any other pleas
"holden within the city.
"Also, that the Hustings shall sit once in a week, on
"Monday, namely.
"Also, that the king will cause the citizens of London to
"have their lands, and securities, and debts, within
"the City and without; and as to lands to which they
"they shall make claim before him, he shall have
"right done unto them according to the laws of the
"City.
"Also, that if any person shall take toll or custom from
"the men of London, the citizens of London, in the
"City, shall take from the Borough or vill, where
"such toll or custom shall have been taken, as much
"as such men of London shall have given for toll, and
"have received in damage therefrom."

It will be observed that these regulations relate chiefly to the administration of justice, civil and criminal, and to local taxation. It has been already stated, in the chapter upon the Borough of Leicester, that the burgesses found the interference of the baronial officers vexatious, and their exactions oppressive, and that in order to avoid these, they stipulated with the earl for the substitution of a gross annual payment to him, undertaking themselves the collecting of the various customs and dues in detail, in place of being at the mercy of an overbearing and unscrupulous bailiff or steward. This is the meaning of the article by which the citizens of London obtained the appointment of one among themselves as sheriff; and this power was extended to the citizens of Norwich. The inhabitants of London also had the appointment of a justiciar or judge from among themselves, to keep the pleas of the Crown, and this privilege was extended to the citizens of Norwich. From this we learn that in the two cities the inhabitants could elect a judge, before whom cases could be heard involving the infliction of the extreme penalty of the law, and the decisions of trials of the gravest importance. In London, the citizens were relieved from the necessity of pleading to any pleas in any court beyond the walls: the like exemption was extended to the citizens of Norwich. The citizens of London were "quit of Scot and Lot, Danegeld and Murder;" and "no one of them" was obliged "to wage battle." This declaration indicates that in London, and by extension to Norwich, the inhabitants were freed from the payment of scot and lot— a custom levied for the use of the sheriff or his bailiff; from an ancient tax levied in the period of the Danish Invasions; and from a payment imposed on the whole community, in case of the discovery of a murder amongst them, committed by an unknown individual. Further, neither in London nor in Norwich were they compelled to fight duels in settling disputed rights to property; thus obtaining the abolition of the Norman usage referred to in previous pages.* In London, in case a citizen was arraigned on some charge of a criminal nature, he could clear himself by

* See pages 39, 40, etc.

the oath of six, eighteen, or thirty-six compurgators—in other words, if he could find that number of citizens to declare their belief in his innocence, he was acquitted; the citizens of Norwich were placed on the same footing in this respect. Occasionally, the vassals and retainers of the king or the barons would quarter themselves by force upon the Londoners; by the charter of Henry they were freed from this intrusion, and the citizens of Norwich were similarly protected therefrom. The men of London and all their goods were quit throughout England, and the seaports, of certain local payments and customs enumerated in the chapter on the Borough of Preston: the same exemption was extended to the people of Norwich. In the two cities some of the principal inhabitants were proprietors of land and houses, having, within separate jurisdictions, authority over their tenants. Sometimes the priests of the churches, at others aldermen (who in London were called "barons"), and occasionally wealthy citizens, had their "sokes," in which they levied "customs" upon the inhabitants. By the charter of Henry the First, it seems that such persons were living in London and Norwich. At this date every man in London had his "were" or pecuniary value, in the estimation of the law; by the same charter it was provided that no man should be fined beyond that amount—that is to say, should not be ruinously "amerced." It is to be inferred that in the law courts designated the "folk-mote" the ends of justice were occasionally defeated by "miskenning" or mis-pleading—a fine being levied for faults or variations made in pleadings; this was abolished in the charters under notice. An ancient court in the city of London was called the Hustings, which took cognizance of a class of causes affecting lands and tenements, rents and services, over which the chief magistrates and sheriff presided; it was conceded by the charter already quoted, that it should be held once in the week, namely, on the Monday. The remaining articles in the London charter are sufficiently clear to render further explanation unnecessary.

Nothing contained in the grants made by Henry the First to London and Norwich relates to the strictly municipal affairs of the citizens. What they seem to have desired was complete independence in respect to the administration of the law, civil and criminal, and local taxation. No allusion is made to the presence of a Merchant's Guild in either of the two cities; yet we cannot doubt that the institution was in existence both in London and Norwich, for no inhabitant of either town would have been considered eligible to enjoy the local privileges, or to carry on trade, unless he were first enrolled as a burgess and found securities for the fulfilment of his obligations; as we have seen was the case in Preston and Leicester. It must therefore be understood as taken for granted that every citizen of London and Norwich, whatever might be his position in reference to legal matters, was united with his fellow-citizens in the fraternity known as the Guild. If no other fact warranted us in this statement, the existence of ancient Guild Halls in the two cities would be sufficient to do so; for what does this imply but that those halls were buildings in which the Guild of the city met, as it met in every borough throughout England? To think of a civic community without its Guild, would in truth be to think of the human body without the vital principle sustaining its activity and progress.

After the date of Henry the First's charter, the government of the city of Norwich was severed from that of the Castle, and the King's two parts of the public dues became the right of the citizens, who were thereafter authorized to exercise all such jurisdiction as the King had ever done in reference to those parts, and they returned their fee farm by their provost or sheriff, chosen by themselves, who accounted yearly for them in the Exchequer.

The age was one, however, of continual change owing to the unsettled relationship between the kings and the barons. This was illustrated in the case of Norwich. King Stephen gave the citizens a new charter, vesting the government of their city in coroners and bailiffs in the room of sheriffs and provosts, but Hugh Bigod (who held the castle of Norwich) being suspected by Henry of a partiality to the cause of Matilda, was dispossessed by him of the Castle, and the citizens at the same time of their liberties. The citizens sued immediately and earnestly that the King would re-grant to them their privileges, which they at last obtained; but they were put under the government of a royal officer, as before. In the year 1130 they paid into the hands of the sheriff twenty-five pounds as a composition aid to the King, for their pardon and the restoration of their liberties. Their fortunes, however, being so intimately connected with those of Hugh Bigod, their liberties were held by a very precarious tenure. Thus, when Bigod openly declared for Matilda in the following year, the privileges of the citizens were again suspended. When the refractory baron returned to his allegiance shortly after, the local liberties were restored to the inhabitants at his intercession, and confirmed by a new charter.

But the citizens were not destined long to retain the election of their own sheriff or provost. They were not allowed to occupy a position so advantageous in a semi-barbarous period. When Hugh Bigod was restored to the dignity and title of Earl of Norfolk, and appointed constable of the castle of Norwich, in the year 1163, he became sole governor of the city then in the king's hands, and its sheriff from that time acted wholly under his authority.

In a previous page it has been related how disastrously the burgesses of Leicester became involved in the fate of their earl, on his taking part in the insurrection originated by Queen Eleanor and her sons against Henry II. At Norwich, at the very same time, the citizens took the opposite course to that pursued by the people of Leicester, for while the latter (probably under compulsion) resisted the arms of their sovereign, the former refused admittance to Hugh Bigod, when he demanded to enter Norwich as a rebel against his sovereign. They suffered in consequence injuries almost as extensive as the townspeople of Leicester; the Earl of Norfolk, provoked at the resistance he met with, plundering the town, burning great part of it, and taking all the principal inhabitants prisoners. But shortly after, the king defeating the insurgents, took the castle and city of Norwich into his own hands—earl Hugh meanwhile departing for the Holy Land and dying there; and for the purpose of making some amends to the citizens, for the damages they had sustained in opposing the earl, the king remitted a large portion of the local taxation of the city in the year 1175. After the lapse of a few years, also, Henry restored to the citizens the liberties which had been withheld from them, from the date of Hugh Bigod's becoming sole governor of the city.

This state of affairs continued until the accession of Roger, son of Hugh Bigod, to the earldom of Norfolk. Richard Cœur de Lion had been five years king when he granted a charter to the citizens, confirming all the concessions which had been made to them by Henry the First. The communal independence of Norwich was now, it seems, secured beyond the possibility of revocation.

While the inhabitants of Norwich had been subject to the repeated disasters already described, they had in addition sustained injuries and offences in another direction.

Not only had they been scourged by king and baron—they had also received stripes of injury from the lordly ecclesiastics of the period; as will be shown in the next chapter.

CHAPTER X.

THE CITY OF NORWICH (CONTINUED).

In tracing the progress of its municipal development, we have omitted to record the erection of a cathedral in the city, some generations before the date at which the narrative has arrived. In the reign of William Rufus, a bishop of the East Angles was living, to whom the popular voice had assigned a name descriptive of his character for flattery, or for a less venial disregard of truth; he was known as Herbert Lozinga, the liar or flatterer. It was commonly reported that he had been guilty of simony in obtaining the episcopal chair. In order to efface this reproach, or to atone for his sin, he built a beautiful edifice in the lower part of the city, near the castle, and translated his see from Thetford to Norwich. The structure became the mother church of Norfolk and Suffolk. On the south side of it, he founded a monastery for sixty monks, whom he liberally endowed with lands for their maintenance, and within certain limits around the church and monastery the bishop obtained exclusive privileges and franchises for the residents, from both regal and papal authorities. In doing this, the bishop aroused the jealousy of the citizens, and disputes arose between them and the monks, which were perpetuated through generation after generation.

A partial subsidence of differences took place in the reign of King John, but they broke out with greater violence than ever in the reign of his son, Henry the Third. The monks, in some way or other not stated in local history incensed the populace to such a degree that they forcibly entered the convent, and plundered and burnt part of it, rendering some interference necessary on behalf of the higher powers. When the sheriff of Norfolk was about to visit the city, to examine the extent of the depredations committed, the burgesses would neither suffer him to do so, nor do it themselves. The king, finding his officer thus resisted, seized all the liberties of the citizens into his own hands; though shortly after, upon their submission, he restored them.

A triumph was nevertheless reserved for the citizens, as, in the year 1244, when the government-tax for the city was laid at one hundred pounds, the tenants of the Prior of Norwich, dwelling in the privileged locality, were taxed at twenty pounds, which they were obliged to pay, though they had hitherto escaped the obligation. This was one result of a visit made to Norwich by Henry the Third, after he had commanded that the citizens should not molest the monks in the lands or places belonging to the convent. The citizens exulted over the fact, that while the Prior had gained a nominal victory over them, they had secured a substantial advantage over him, in placing his tenants on the same footing as they themselves were with respect to the taxgatherer.

Fuel seemed never wanting to keep in a blaze the fire of animosity enkindled between the two parties. When the barons rose in arms against King Henry the Third, with Simon de Montfort at their head, the bishop and clergy took their side; while the City bailiffs and commons, with the dwellers in the castle fee declared for the monarch. The leader of the barons enlisted in his favour Roger Bigod, earl of Norfolk, who was constable of Norwich Castle, and thus the citizens were overawed; but when the king defeated the insurgent barons at Evesham, he removed Roger Bigod from his office, and appointed in his place John de Vaux. While these feuds prevailed, many lives of the monks and their partisans were taken by the citizens, and they in their turn suffered by the retaliation of their opponents, and the two factions burned down each others' houses. About the middle of December, 1266, the barons, headed by Sir John d'Eyville, entered the city, and killed and imprisoned a great number of the inhabitants, carrying away with them in triumph some of the wealthier citizens. The year following, the bailiffs being summoned to answer for the many murders and disorders lately committed in Norwich, contemptiously departed from the court without leave, and the king in consequence seized their liberties and kept them in his own hands.

The citizens and the monks were embittered against each other by these frequent armed collisions; so that they scarcely needed a pretext for attacking each other with their weapons, on any public occasion. On Trinity Sunday, in the year 1272, a fair was held according to custom, under the authority of a charter granted to the monks, before the gates of the monastery. It was attended by the citizens and the servants of the monks; and as might have been expected, they came to blows, the lives of several of the former being taken in the affray. Warrants were directly issued, in consequence of the city coroner's inquest, for the apprehension of the murderers wherever they could be taken. This touched the pride of the monks, who held that the officers of the city magistrates had no right to enter within their jurisdiction in pursuit of the criminals, as it was exempt from the interference of the authorities. They accordingly shut up their gates, and enlisted the services of a body of soldiers, who shot at and wounded with their missles several passers-by belonging to the city. They did not confine themselves to these outrages, as on the Sunday before St. Lawrence's day (August 10) they rushed into the city, which they ravaged all that day and night, plundering the houses and killing several merchants and citizens. In this emergency, the magistrates despatched letters to the king, relating the proceedings which had occurred, and summoned the citizens to meet them in the Market-place on the day following. The inhabitants rose in a body, and, enraged at the brutal excesses committed by the myrmidons of the church, they flew to the Priory, assaulted it on every side, set fire to the great gates, and stormed its defences. Once within, they applied the torch to St. Albert's church, the great Almonry, the church doors, and the great tower, which was speedily enwrapped in the flames and burnt down, as far as the materials allowed. The whole church (except St. Mary's chapel), with the dormitory, refectory, hall of entertainment and infirmary (with its chapel), and almost all the buildings in the court, were consumed. Of the dwellers in the precincts, many of the sub-deacons, clerks, and some laymen, were dispatched in the cloister and precincts of the monastery; others were carried out and put to the sword in the city; and others cast into prison. All the plate, holy vessels, books, and vestments, and what articles the flames had not destroyed in the church, were carried off by the besiegers, and for three days they slew and plundered without scruple or mercy the tenants and partizans of the ecclesiastics. The prior fled meanwhile to Yarmouth, and the monks who survived sought refuge wherever it was to be obtained.

The report of this outrage reached the ears of Henry the Third, who convened a meeting of all the nobles and bishops of England, at Bury St. Edmund's, on St. Giles's day, to take into consideration what should be done in reference to so important a matter. Simultaneously the Bishop of Norwich called the clergy together at Eye in Suffolk; when excommunication was denounced against all persons concerned in the acts here described, and the whole city was placed under interdict—the effect being a suspension of all religious ceremonies, as those in relation to the burial of the dead, the marriage service, and the performing of mass and vespers. All commerce and business was also necessarily suspended, and confusion everywhere existed. The whole power of church and state was in truth brought to bear upon the unfortunate citizens of Norwich, and with brutal accompaniments, as will be shortly related. The barons, most of whom held in partial dependence boroughs of their own, and the bishops who feared perhaps the manifestation in the localities of their own sees a spirit of rebellion like that so audaciously exhibited at Norwich, were not likely to counsel moderation in dealing with the offenders. The result of the Parliament at Bury, was the visit of the king in person to the scene of the insurrection, with the intention sternly to punish the rebels. He entered the city on September 14, when, at his request, the bishop removed the interdict. Then followed atrocities which seem incredible in these days. The king's justices caused thirty-four of the offenders to be drawn by horses through the streets until they were dead; others were hanged and quartered, and their bodies afterwards burned; and a woman who first set fire to the gates was burnt alive! Minor penalties were inflicted on the remainder of those who were implicated in the transactions already described. Twelve of the inhabitants forfeited their goods to the king. The city was fined 3,000 marks towards re-building the cathedral, and £100 for a cup weighing ten pounds in gold. The king also seized the city and its liberties, and assigned officials to govern it in his name. At the same time, the prior (to whom some of the blame arising out of these troubles was ascribed) was committed to the episcopal dungeon; his manors and the priory property being taken out of his hands by the offended monarch.

The citizens—in whom it is impossible not to see some of the spirit of their hardy ancestors, the Norsemen—refused to pay the sum which they had been amerced for damages; and the bishop again laid the city under interdict. In this state Norwich remained until 1274—the interdict being removed and re-imposed in the interval—the citizens continuing still stubborn and resentful. The prior and convent demanded of them four thousand marks for damages. In November, two of the monks were sent to Rome, with an account of the whole matter; complaining of the citizens, and citing them to appear and answer in the pope's court. The pope, however, delegated the matter for trial to the bishops of Ely and London; but, at the outset, the latter personage dying, it was again referred to the pope, who left the sole decision to the king; and the dispute was finally settled. These were the terms of agreement. The citizens, within the space of six years, were to pay the sum of 3,000 marks towards re-building the cathedral, and give to the use of the high altar a pyx or cup weighing ten pounds in gold, and worth one hundred pounds in money. The monks were to make new gates to their monastery, and go into the city, injuring no man in his property. And, by way of completion of the affair, some of the chief citizens, at their own charge, were to make a journey to Rome, to assure the pope of the truth of this agreement, and humbly to beg his pardon and peace. The conditions were complied with, and then the king restored the city to all its ancient privileges and liberties; but at the same time he commanded that the treasurer of the city should pay yearly into his exchequer forty shillings over and above the old fee-farm, as a penalty, and in perpetual remembrance of the event. The bishop raised the interdict in November 1275, and in the following year the pope's general absolution, which had arrived from Rome, was published in the city by order of the archbishop of Canterbury.

CHAPTER XI.

THE CITY OF NORWICH (CONCLUDED).

While attempting to describe the feud between the monks and citizens, we have, for the time, dropped the thread of the narrative of the purely municipal development of the borough, and therefore here resume it in due order. The charter of Richard Cœur de Lion established the burgesses in the possession of their privileges, though the latter were from time to time suspended (as the last chapter shows), at the discretion of the various monarchs. Henry the Third granted three charters; but they do not seem to have added any material franchises to those already possessed by the burgesses. In one he empowered them to enclose their city with a ditch. In his third charter, bearing date 1256, he gave them the return of all writs, as well as of summons out of the exchequer, as of all other things relating to the city of Norwich; requiring also that all merchants, enjoying their liberties and merchandizes, should pay to the lot, scot, and aids of the citizens, wherever they might dwell, as they ought and used to do; and that, for the future, no guild be held in the city to its damage.

We here perceive that, as the inhabitants of the Bishop's Fee, near Leicester, were called on to contribute their quota to local taxation, though living outside the borough, the merchants of Norwich, wherever dwelling, were required to do the same thing—the inference being that for some time previously a portion of the suburban population had participated in local advantages without sharing the public burdens.

The concluding clause of this charter has been construed to imply the abolition of the Guild Merchant, subsequently to the date mentioned. But it appears to show that at least a Guild had previously existed, as it requires that "*in future* no Guild be held in the city," while the qualifying words, "to its damage," may be taken to signify that if the institution were carried on to the public benefit, it might be allowed to continue in existence.

During the reigns of the three Edwards, Norwich seems to have been left in the enjoyment of some tranquillity, after having endured so many wrongs at the hands of the Norman monarchs and the ecclesiastics of the locality. The liberties of the citizens were undisturbed, and monarch after monarch confirmed them in a formal way in their charters. In the fourteenth century, the commercial condition of the city was greatly and rapidly improved. In 1331 the king constituted it a staple town for the counties of Norfolk and Suffolk, and therefore wool, sheepskins, and other commodities were taken there exclusively for sale. Five years after, great numbers of Flemings settled in this city and elsewhere, under the protection of Edward the Third's queen, Philippa; in consequence of which, in a few years, it became the most flourishing place in England, through its extensive trade in worsteds, fustians, pieces, and other woollen manufactures. Local history speaks of its sixty parish churches, besides seven attached to convents, within the walls; and when the great plague broke out in 1348, it is recorded fifty-seven thousand persons, exclusive of the dwellers in the convents and beggars, fell victims in one year to its ravages. And, two years after, the city was so far recovered, that a great tournament was held in it, at which Edward the Black Prince was present, with many of the nobility, and they were sumptuously entertained by the local authorities.

When Richard the Second ascended the throne, he granted a charter to the citizens, confirming all its former rights, and containing additional clauses. As the people of Norwich always claimed to be on a footing of equality with their contemporaries, they obtained an exemplification, under the crown seal, of the last charter granted to the citizens of London in the year 1337, for the purpose of being properly informed as to the extent of metropolitan privileges; but no addition appears to have been made to those of the people of Norwich.

The city was now rapidly prospering, and was visited by the most distinguished personages in the state, to many of whom loans were advanced. Its walls and towers were kept in a condition of completeness and repair, and constantly guarded, and the political influence of the citizens was felt and recognized throughout the country. When John of Gaunt visited them in 1389, they received him with the highest honours; and ten years after they openly espoused the cause of the House of Lancaster, by declaring themselves for his son, afterwards crowned Henry the Fourth.

The citizens had not hitherto been governed by a Mayor. They had so long been ruled by royal provosts that they earnestly desired to appoint their own chief magistrate. In response to their appeals, Henry had given them strong assurances that whenever it was in his power he would grant them a charter, enabling them to elect their Mayors. On obtaining the crown, therefore, he fulfilled his promise, and in the year 1403 conceded to them the much-coveted authority. By this charter the office of bailiff was abolished, and the citizens were authorised to elect a Mayor yearly; and two sheriffs for the city and its county, to be sworn by the mayor in the Guildhall, and their names returned into Chancery. The sheriffs were to hold their county courts from month to month, and have the same liberties and privileges as the sheriffs of counties had, and were to receive the profits thence accruing. No citizen was to plead or be impleaded for or concerning any lands in any court out of the bounds of the city and its county; nor for any bargain made or fault committed within those bounds; neither were the king's justices to enter, or concern themselves in anything thereto belonging, but all should be done before the mayor and sheriffs according to the law and customs of the city. The citizens and commonalty were to have cognizance of all pleas, assizes, and of all lands and tenements in the city and its county; as well as of those pleas that were triable before the justices of both benches, justices of assize, or justices itinerant; all which should be tried before the mayor and sheriffs in the Guildhall.—Into further details of this charter it is scarcely needful to enter, sufficient having been given to show that, as far as possible under the circumstances, the king conferred upon the city an independent civil and criminal jurisdiction. The great authority imparted to the mayor is apparent. He was placed above the sheriffs, and he could determine any case of felony with the king's special mandate. The king having presented the city with a sword, it was to be carried before the mayor and sheriffs, with the point erect, in the presence of all lords or nobles of the realm, though not in the presence of the king or his successors. The serjeants-at-mace were to carry gold or silver maces before the mayor and sheriffs, with the king's arms engraved thereon, in the king's presence, and that of the queen-consort, or queen-mother in the city and its county.

When the charter arrived in Norwich, it was received with great demonstrations of joy; being evidently considered an act of civic elevation of unprecedented importance; and in pursuance of its leading provision, on the 1st of May they elected William Appelton their first Mayor, and in Michaelmas following Robert Brasier and John Daniel their Sheriffs. But the receipt of the new charter was followed by disputes between the commons and the Mayor and his Council, relative to the modes of electing officers and the exercise of other powers, which led to the demand for another charter, granted by Henry the Fifth, in 1418, in which all former grants were recited at large and confirmed, and some new liberties were added.

The same love of pageantry which has been shown to have existed in Preston, and which existed in other ancient boroughs, manifested itself in Norwich; where, under the authority of a charter of Henry the Fifth, granted in 1417, the members of the religious fraternities called "Guilds," who had previously held their "ridings" or "processions," carried them on with greater pomp and on a more extensive scale than before. The Guild of St. George, with the trade fraternities, revelled in all the splendours of medieval show on such occasions. These festivities, however, were associated with the Church, and were not affairs in which the municipal authorities by virtue of their offices took any part; though the chief functionaries of the city by their presence showed their reverence for their religion and its priests. The Tuesday before the eve of John the Baptist's day was the day of the inauguration of the Mayor elect, when there was an annual procession, fairly rivalling a similar festivity in London. First in order was the figure of a green dragon, with four attendants bearing drawn swords, and then in succession followed the Mayor and Aldermen, and inferior personages, with music and banners, and all the accompaniments of the occasion. The whole of the members of the procession went to the cathedral, where they attended the services, after which they repaired to their ancient Hall, within whose walls the civic dignitaries and their friends were entertained at a sumptuous banquet.

In the great contest of the fifteenth century, commonly called the "Wars of the Roses," the citizens of Norwich adhered firmly to the cause of the House of Lancaster; as might have been expected from them after the concession of the Charter they so much desired by Henry the Fourth. When his son was on the eve of departure for France, they lent him one thousand marks. The sixth Henry twice visited the city, and was entertained at the public expense. His queen (Margaret) being terrified at the rumour of the advance of Edward, Earl of March, towards London, besought the aid of the inhabitants; when the commons resolved to lend one hundred marks to the king, and the aldermen presented the queen with sixty marks, to which the commons added forty more. In the year 1460, the mayor and aldermen raised forty armed men—the commons eighty—for the service of Henry the Sixth. The fidelity of a large community to its sovereigns, evidenced during more than sixty years, is here remarkably exemplified.

Such, however, was the force of political necessity, that the Norwich citizens found it expedient to make their peace with the Yorkist monarch, Edward the Fourth, who granted a charter to them, dividing Norwich from the rest of the county of Norfolk, and making it a county of itself; but it did not incorporate the inhabitants. It provided for the election of aldermen and common councilmen, and of a mayor and two sheriffs by them; and jurisdiction was given to the mayor, sheriffs, and commonalty over all real and personal actions within the borough. But (as remarked by an authority on this subject *) "this is a striking instance, after incorporation had been introduced, of a grant of all the usual privileges accompanying the exclusive jurisdiction of a borough, without any grant of incorporation."

* The History of Boroughs by Messrs. Merewether and Stephens.

In the two centuries following this date, the municipal history offers no event which requires record; though there were many political struggles, as in the insurrection of Kett, and the war between the King and Parliament, in which the citizens participated, in the latter case ranging themselves on the side of the Parliament.

The city was not incorporated in the reign of Elizabeth, when, as already explained, so many boroughs received charters of incorporation; but in the time of Charles the Second, shortly after the Restoration, its form of government was settled, on the foundation on which it remained until the reign of William the Fourth. Under the charter of Charles, the mayor, recorder, and steward for the time being, with all such aldermen as had been mayors, were constituted justices of the peace in the city and county, and in their respective wards; the election of sheriffs and aldermen was regulated; and the power of making laws, orders, and constitutions for the better regulation, and holding courts of equity and pleas, was conceded. The citizens were at the same time incorporated with the usual corporate powers.

James, Duke of York, visited the city in the year 1681, and it would seem succeeded in impressing the authorities with a feeling of loyalty to the Stuarts which overcame their discretion. An address was forwarded by them to Charles the Second, in consequence, which in its assertion of the royal prerogative exceeded any other, and was presented at the king's bench as a public libel by the grand jury of Middlesex. Yet farther did the ruling body carry their infatuation; as in the year 1682 they surrendered their charter into the king's hands by a majority of forty against twenty-two, with the remonstrances of nine hundred citizens against the proceeding. The promoters of the movement alleged that they had received assurances another charter, granting larger immunities and more extended privileges, would be given to them; but when they obtained it their mistake was apparent—for, instead of providing them with the promised advantages, it contained a remarkable clause, whereby the king reserved to himself a power to displace any magistrate who should make himself obnoxious to royal prerogative, by signifying his pleasure under his privy seal.

Under this charter, Robert Paston, earl of Yarmouth lord lieutenant of Norfolk and Norwich, was appointed Recorder. He was succeeded by his son, William, earl of Yarmouth, who, at an assembly held on the 19th day of July, produced letters-patent under the great seal of England, empowering him to appoint a deputy recorder; and he therefore nominated John Warkehouse, Esq. to that office. The assembly, looking on this as a violation of the ancient liberties of the city, and contrary to the express sense and meaning of their new charter, resolved to petition the king thereupon, but they could obtain no redress. They were obliged to submit, and to swear Mr. Warkehouse as the deputy recorder.

With that arbitrary spirit which cost the second James his sceptre, he displaced nineteen members of the common council and ten aldermen; but on the issuing forth of a proclamation by him, when William, prince of Orange, was on his way to the shores of this island, they were restored to their respective offices. From that time to the date of the passing of the Municipal Reform Act, the municipal constitution of the city remained unchanged; and then the new system was introduced which is now in operation.

CHAPTER XII.

THE BOROUGH OF YARMOUTH.

When the Romans were dwelling in this island, the present site of Yarmouth was under the waves of the German Ocean. In the reign of king Edward the Confessor, the sands began to come into view at low water. There were then seventy burgesses settled on the site. Afterwards, in the time of William the Conqueror, the sands became dry and elevated, and people began to resort to them, and placed booths on them in which to entertain the merchants, seafaring-men, and fishermen, of this country, and France and the Low Countries; especially between Michaelmas and Martinmas every year, when a great trade was carried on in herrings. In the reign of William Rufus, Herbert, bishop of Norwich (who has been mentioned in a preceding chapter) erected on the shore a chapel, where the fishermen could pay their devotions; and in succeeding reigns, in the twelfth century, the ground had acquired such solidity that the multitude of persons who flocked to the spot began to build houses and dwelling-places thereon. Henry the First appointed a provost or governor of the place, and the bishop of Norwich founded a church there in honour of God, and of Nicholas, the patron saint of sailors and fishermen. In this state matters remained during the reigns of Henry the First, Stephen, Henry the Second, and Richard the First, for nearly a century, until the time of John, who, says an ancient writer,* "consideringe the place and scituation verye meete to be buylded and resorted unto by manye other nations as well as by the people of this land, and intending to provide for the good government of the

---

* Henry Manship, formerly Town Clerk of Yarmouth, whose Manuscript has been published by Mr. Palmer, F.S.A.; the Author also of a History of Great Yarmouth, 2 vols. quarto, 1856.

same, did determine to create the place and scituation into a Free Borough, the whiche had been governed by the king's provoste in the time of the said fower last kinges." From its proximity to the mouth of the river Yare, the place became known as "Yarmouth."

The charter which king John granted to the inhabitants being the first conferred upon them, and including every privilege which it may be presumed they could obtain, is important, as discovering the exact municipal position they occupied at that period. It is therefore here copied in full:*

"John, by the grace of God, king of England, lord of
"Ireland, duke of Normandy and Aquitain, and earl
"of Anjou; to the Archbishops, Bishops, Abbots,
"Priors, Earls, Barons, Justices, Sheriffs, Provosts, and
"to all Bailiffs, and others his faithful subjects, greet-
"ing. Know ye that we have granted, and by our
"present Charter, confirmed, to our Burgesses at Yar-
"mouth, that they have, the Burgh of Yarmouth in
"fee farm for ever; and that the Burgh be a Free
"Burgh for ever; and have soc and sac, toll and
"theam, and infangenthief and outfangenthief. And
"that the same Burgesses through our Land, and
"through all the Sea Ports, be quit of toll, lastage,
"passage, pavage, pontage, stallage, and of leve, and
"of danegeld, and of every other custom, saving the
"liberty of the city of London'; and that they do no
"suit of counties, or hundreds, for tenures within the
"Burgh of Yarmouth.

"We have also granted to the same burgesses, and by
"this our charter have confirmed, that none of them
"plead out of the Burgh of Yarmouth, in any plea,

---

* Palmer's *History of Norwich*, pp. 2 and 3. See also Parkyns' *History of Yarmouth*, pp. 134, 135, 136, 137, and 138.

"except the plea of outward tenures. We have also
"granted to them acquittance of murder within the
"burgh of Yarmouth; and that none of them shall
"fight the combat. And that they may try the pleas
"of the crown amongst themselves, according to the
"law and custom of Oxford. And that within the
"burgh aforesaid, none shall take quarters by force,
"or by assignment of the marshals. And in that
"burgh there shall be no plea of *miskenning;* and that
"be holden but once a week. We have also granted
"to them a Merchant Guild; and that they shall justly
"have their lands and tenures, their securities, and all
"their debts, which any one shall owe them. And
"concerning their lands and tenures, which are within
"the burgh aforesaid, according to the law and custom
"of the burgh of Oxford: and concerning all their
"debts, which shall be contracted at Yarmouth, and
"securities made there, the pleas shall be held at Yar-
"mouth. And if any one in all England, shall take
"tolls or custom from the burgesses of Yarmouth
"except, as above, the said city of London; and after-
"wards that person shall fail to assert his right, the
"provost of Yarmouth shall take out the writ of
"Naam at Yarmouth.
"Moreover, for the amendment of the said burgh of Yar-
"mouth, we have granted, that whatever merchants
"shall come to the burgh of Yarmouth with their
"wares, of whatever place they shall be, whether
"foreigners or otherwise, who are at peace with us, or
"by our permission shall come into our land, they
"may come, stay, and depart in our safe peace, on
"paying the right customs of that burgh. We also
"prohibit that any one injure, or damage, or molest
"the aforesaid burgesses, upon forfeiture of ten
"pounds.

"Wherefore, we will and strictly command, that the
"aforesaid burgesses of Yarmouth, and their heirs,
"have and hold for ever all the franchises aforesaid,
"hereditarily, truly, and peaceably, freely, quietly, and
"wholly, fully and honourably, on paying thereout
"annually fifty and five pounds by tail, by the hand
"of the provost of Yarmouth, into our Exchequer, at
"the term of St Michael.

"And the burgesses of Yarmouth shall yearly choose
"such provosts out of themselves, as shall be agree-
"able to us and to them."

[Here follow the names of the witnesses, and the date of the charter, March 18, 1208.]

On comparison of the contents of this charter with those of charters already referred to in previous chapters, the same general purposes will seem to have been aimed at by the inhabitants of Yarmouth, as by their contemporaries in the other towns of the country, namely, the establishment of their own collective local authority independently of any other authority, whether it was that of the crown, or the neighbouring baron, or the county officers, in reference to civil and criminal administration; the management of their own municipal affairs by the instrumentality of their Guild Merchant; exemption from the payment of all taxes and customs except those necessary to defray local expenses; and the commutation of the various royal dues into one fixed annual payment to the monarch, collected by their own bailiff. It was by these measures the townsmen of Yarmouth rendered it a "free borough"—free from external interference as far as possible. They paid fifty-five pounds' weight of silver into the king's exchequer, every Michaelmas, by the hands of the provost, chosen from their own body, and then they were at liberty to settle the law among themselves—to make the debtor pay his debts, to punish the thief, and to hang the murderer; and to manage all other local affairs, such as the admission to their ranks, as participators in their freedom and privileges, of strangers and others—the levying of taxes for common purposes—the regulation of their commercial dealings with each other, and with the burgesses of other towns—and other kindred matters. In this way they united (as described at pages 12 and 13) the powers of the Court Leet and the Merchants Guild.

For more than two generations this simple form of commonwealth served the purposes of the inhabitants of Yarmouth; but they found, as their affairs made progress, that they required other arrangements better adapted to their altered position. They therefore laid before Henry the Third a set of articles, or bye-laws, by which they solicited to be governed, and which he confirmed by his letters patent, dated Oct. 26, in the 56th year of his reign. Under these bye-laws were yearly elected "four wise men," who were the bailiffs, and to them the government of the place was entrusted. They were to be assisted by twenty-four persons, called "Jurats"—that is, *jurati*, or sworn officers, who were chosen by the burgesses generally. They were in subsequent times called "aldermen." The nature of the oath taken by these "Jurats" is already stated in the fifth chapter of this Essay,[*] in which the arrangements of the Merchant Guild of Leicester are described. The Jurat, by his oath, bound himself in the presence of the chief officers and brethren of the Guild to render justice to the poor as well as the rich; to regularly attend the town assembly; to obey the summons of his superior officers; to maintain the assize of bread, wine, and beer; and maintain the franchise and customs of the town,—calling on God and his saints to help him in the discharge of his duties.

[*] See p. 56.

This constitution remained in existence for centuries, being confirmed by successive monarchs under the Great Seal of England. In the reign of Edward the First, the Jurats compiled a code of the local laws and customs, a translation of which is still extant. By an ordinance of the body, made in the 10th year of Richard the Second, it seems that they chose all the officers of the borough—the bailiffs, chamberlains, managers, collectors, and so forth.*

In the reign of Richard the Second (1379) the courts called "Leets," of the borough, were in regular operation.† The same court sat in four different parts of the town upon different days, for the local convenience of the inhabitants, and was presided over by the four bailiffs. A jury of twelve inhabitants was sworn, by whom offences were tried. If a person bought and sold in the town as a burgess, when he was not so, he was fined for so doing. A woman claimed to be of the liberty of Yarmouth, but was not a burgess; she was therefore fined. The circumstance was continually recurring of inhabitants buying and selling, not being burgesses, and being subject to penalties for persisting in that course. An inhabitant, not being a burgess, was presented before the Court for binding apprentices, and was fined accordingly.

From these instances, it is shown, that before any person was entitled to buy and sell, or to take apprentices, in Yarmouth, he must be a "burgess." What this implied at Leicester and Preston, we have already seen. At the former place, no person was allowed to trade unless he had entered the Merchant Guild; he was liable to a fine if he did so, and every member of the Guild by his oath was pledged to inform the Mayor of any inhabitant not being in the Guild who bought and sold, in order that such a one might be

* Parkyns' History, pp. 138 to 143.

† Merrywether and Stephens' *History of Boroughs*, pp. 753—759.

prevented from persisting in that course of proceeding. In Preston, none were allowed to "make any merchandize" —that is, to carry on trade—unless they were members of the Guild Merchant: they were not held to be "burgesses" until they had entered that association. It would therefore seem that at Yarmouth, as at Preston and Lancaster, no man could be held to be a "burgess," in the fullest sense of the word, unless he were a Guildman; though he might be within the jurisdiction of the Court Leet, in respect to civil processes and criminal administration.

At a subsequent date, the necessity of enlarging the ruling body was discovered, and then a number of common-councilmen were added to the aldermen. In the reign of Henry the Fourth, the practice of electing two bailiffs instead of four was introduced, and at the same time forty-eight common-councilmen were united in the government of the town with the bailiffs and aldermen. In this state the municipal system continued until the reign of Charles the First, when an agitation began in favour of a change, chiefly in regard to the principal officers of the borough.

At first, under the charter of King John, the burgesses elected one provost yearly; then they appointed four bailiffs; and finally they chose two. In the second year of Charles the First a formal complaint was made, at an assembly of the municipal body, held in July, that several of its members had projected a scheme for substituting a mayor for the two bailiffs. On a motion being proposed in its favour, the majority rejected it; resolving that if any one of that society should thereafter presume to introduce such a proposal, he should be immediately expelled from it, as an unworthy member. A division ensued, accompanied by the dismissal of several persons—among the rest of a Mr. Alderman Neve, in whose place was chosen Thomas

Green. A representation of the proceeding being made to the king, he despatched a letter to the bailiffs and aldermen requesting them to reverse the procedure, and restore the degraded alderman to his office, and to remove his newly-made successor. The case did not terminate here, however; for having been referred to the privy-council, and by them to some resident gentlemen, the original decision of the municipal assembly was confirmed; Ald. Neve's expulsion being decreed to be final and complete, on the plea of his being a man of unprincipled and litigious character. But the real reason was, that he had proposed an innovation unacceptable to his colleagues.

This act did not close the controversy. On the contrary, it roused the partizans of the new proposal to increased activity; and a bitter and prolonged struggle ensued. A charter was drawn up by the Attorney-general, at the instance of a leading townsman, providing for the appointment of a Mayor, a Recorder, twelve Aldermen, and twenty-four Common-councilmen; with a Sword-bearer, and two Sergeants-at-Mace, to go before the Mayor and other officers, as before; but this was set aside, and it was not until more than fifty years had elapsed that the innovators succeeded in their object. In the year 1684 Charles the Second, in the 36th year of his reign, granted a charter to the inhabitants; incorporating them by the name of the Mayor, Aldermen, Burgesses, and Commonalty of the borough of Yarmouth; the document being modelled upon that which had been previously rejected. The Corporation was to consist of a Mayor, eighteen Aldermen, and thirty-six Common Councilmen. This form of government, however, remained only a short time in being; a general proclamation in the reign of James the First restoring the ancient system, with its Bailiffs and Aldermen as before. In the reign of Queen Anne, the Corporation were as anxious to

supersede their Bailiffs by a Mayor as they had previously
been opposed to the project, and they petitioned the Queen
to grant them a new charter enabling them to carry out
their design. Their prayer was complied with, and the
inhabitants were thenceforward governed by a Mayor,
eighteen Aldermen, and thirty-six Common Councilmen.

In this condition the municipality remained until the
reign of William the Fourth, when Yarmouth became
subject to the new law regulating the Corporations of this
country.

CHAPTER XIII.

ON MARKET TOWNS NOT INCORPORATED.

Throughout England towns are in existence where no corporations are in operation, which, however, have long had, in certain respects, independent jurisdiction and a measure of self-government. In some cases, perhaps in most, the communities in these places have enjoyed for many generations the use and benefit of property belonging to them, and managed on their behalf by trustees or feoffees. To apply the term "municipal" to their institutions would be, in some degree, an inaccuracy, yet the semblance of local freedom and individuality they present entitles them to notice in an Essay like the present.

The author here introduces a few examples of the kind, selected from those with which he is acquainted; because he believes them to be typical of the class existing throughout the country.

Melton Mowbray, at this day a place of resort for fox-hunting, is a market town, situate in the north-eastern part of the county of Leicester. The number of the population is nearly 5,000. To them belong a Town Estate and Market Tolls, which produce £800 yearly; that being applied to the paving, watching, lighting, and improving the town, and the maintenance of the free schools, the fire engines, and the water supply. The estate does not come under the designation of a charity; having been acquired at an ancient date, in the same way as the estates of many boroughs were; as will be explained hereafter. It will be seen shortly that the estate may be placed in the same category as that which is usually termed "municipal" property. The inhabitants have, however, never been incorporated, and the extent to which they have been self-governed has always been limited. The history of the place, in regard to these points, briefly told, will show their position in the past.

At the time of the Doomsday survey, Melton was the centre of a group of hamlets, of which it was the principal. Shortly after the Norman Conquest, it passed into the hands of the family of the Mowbrays, by whom it was held for many generations. Early in the fourteenth century, a small body of Cluniac monks, dependent on the Priory of Lewes, had a cell here, and were endowed with rents derived from local property; the Knights Hospitallers having previously held land in the lordship, and built a chapel on their property, still known as the "Spital End." At a later date, the place was called on to send members to parliament—a circumstance implying that its inhabitants were held to be in the position of burgesses, and able to contribute to the taxation of the country. At what exact date is not known, but assuredly not later than the fifteenth century, two religious fraternities or Guilds were founded in the place, the object of which was the maintenance of priests to say prayers for the souls of the deceased brethren and sisters. One was dedicated to the Virgin Mary; the other to St. John; and to each belonged an altar in the parish church. Two pieces of land, called "Our Lady's Meadow," and "Our Lady's Close," belonged to the "Guild of our Lady the Virgin;" while two or three "wongs" in Melton fields, with various shops and houses in the town, were the property of St. John's Guild. On the suppression of the religious houses and chantries in the reign of Henry the Eighth, the priests were dismissed from their offices, and the purposes for which the revenues were originally bestowed were pronounced superstitious.

At Melton Mowbray, a similar process to that which was carried on throughout the country, with respect to the property of these fraternities, was pursued. In the reign of Edward the Sixth, the churchwardens, on behalf of the town, purchased the property of the Hospitallers (which had been merged in the possessions of St. Mary's Guild, some time previous to the Reformation), and conveyed it to trustees, to provide for the maintenance of the master of the Grammar School of the place. From ancient documents, still extant, we learn that the property of the Monastery of Lewes, called the Spinneys, passed from the Monastery to the hands of Thomas, Lord Cromwell, and on his attainder to Richard Robson, in the sixth year of the reign of Elizabeth. In the same year Richard Robson conveyed the property to three inhabitants of Melton Mowbray, on behalf of the entire body of townsmen. It was then applied to public uses; the householders, "artificers, cottagers, and craftsmen" being allowed to depasture cows on the land, in return for certain moderate annual payments. In the fifteenth year of Elizabeth, it was arranged that certain parcels of the land should become and remain for ever a free cattle pasture for all the inhabitants, and that the timber should be cut down for their common advantage. At the same time certain officers, called Town Wardens, were in existence, to whom was entrusted the letting of the Spinneys and the practical management of the property, for the benefit of the whole of the inhabitants, including the power of sueing or impleading any person for trespass or any other matter; subject, in certain cases, to the concurrence of ten or twelve of the principal men of the parish. The property was invested in four feoffees, on the decease of any of whom their successors were to be appointed, at the wish of ten or twelve of the inhabitants of the "best estimation." In the thirty-ninth year of Elizabeth, Edward Pate remised unto two inhabitants fifty-four acres of pasture land, called Orgar Leys; and in the forty-third year of the same sovereign, the two inhabitants in question enfeoffed nine other inhabitants in the Spinneys—in a meadow lying near the same—in the Orgar Leys—and in certain messuages, cottages, lands, and tenements, which appear to have been those formerly belonging to the two dissolved Guilds; to be applied in the manner prescribed in the deed of the fifteenth year of the reign of Elizabeth—the power of the Town Wardens, in letting and managing, to extend over the additional property acquired under the deed-poll of Edward Pate.

In the year 1628, the management of the town property was placed on a more defined basis than before. The surviving trustees then, with the consent of the inhabitants, enfeoffed nine of the latter in the whole of the parish property, as already mentioned, after reciting that the revenues had always formerly been employed for the public and general use of the town; part in the wages and maintenance of a schoolmaster, and the residue in other public uses, and "in the discharge of the town charges." The election of two Town Wardens, by the feoffees and ten of the chief inhabitants, was also specially mentioned; the Wardens to have the power to sue and implead, to let the Spinneys (as before mentioned), and to receive all the rents, which ten or more of the inhabitants "of the best estimation," jointly with the feoffees, were to dispose of at their discretion.

The system here described remained in operation for several generations. In the year 1759-60, however, an act of parliament was passed for inclosing the open and common fields of Melton Mowbray; and certain commissioners were appointed to carry the act into execution; before whom the surviving trustees laid what was alleged to be a true account of the town property, making no claim for the Spinneys and Ongar Leys, which they suffered the commissioners to divide among the inhabitants at large, to the personal advantage of the trustees, who, in consequence, received larger allotments for themselves, as landowners, than they would have done had they made such claims, as trustees for the town property, as they ought to have advanced. When, in the year 1775, the number of the trustees who had been parties to the proceedings just noticed, had been diminished by the decease of the majority, and it was found necessary to re-constitute the body, the remaining trustees, on the nomination of inhabitants of Melton Mowbray, under their direct influence, appointed a fresh list of trustees, to whom they passed all the town property except the Spinneys and the Orgar Leys, which had been diverted by the commissioners as before stated. The old trustees also altered the mode of electing the Town Wardens, of controlling the accounts and receipts, and of electing new trustees: one of the trustees taking upon himself, chiefly, the management of local affairs, and the trustees frequently choosing two of their own body, without asking for the consent thereto of ten or twelve of the principal inhabitants, and continuing them in office year after year without change; in consequence of which the estate was let to individuals at much less than the proper value, and one of the Wardens took into his own hands a field refusing to show any title in justification of his possession.

These transactions produced great dissatisfaction among the inhabitants generally, and demands were made upon the peccant trustees to render retribution in respect to the property and moneys they had unjustly appropriated to themselves. The appeal however was fruitless. A meeting of inhabitants was accordingly held in the year 1786, in the Town Hall, to take proceedings in the matter; when a nobleman resident in the locality, who had married a daughter of the chief delinquent among the trustees, surrendered a collection of missing deeds. A bill was subsequently filed in Chancery, of which the objects were a strict and thorough enquiry into the proceedings of the trustees appointed in 1775, and an enforced restitution of the property and moneys taken by them from the inhabitants.

The result was a compromise, effected between the two parties before a decree was made by the Court of Chancery. It will have been noticed that the Town Estate, on its acquisition after the Reformation, was managed by the Trustees, Town Wardens, and ten or twelve Inhabitants " of the best estimation." By the terms of the compromise (dated 1793), agreed to without the authority of any Court, and acted upon up to the present day, the management of the Town Estate was thrown open to "all and every of the inhabitants at a meeting to be assembled."

In this way a system was established which was thoroughly democratic, but which in practice proved very inconvenient and troublesome. A few instances of its operation will prove how it operated. The Grammar School being subject to the control of a meeting of inhabitants, on one occasion they were divided on the question of the teaching of the Church Catechism to the scholars, and a poll was taken; on another, a dispute arose as to the propriety of holding the beast and other markets in the town streets, or removing them to a field outside the town. In these small controversies all the fury of party passion was aroused; and in consequence, the professional men and principal tradesmen being exposed to personal obloquy and coarse abuse, left the local administration to inhabitants of inferior position and education. Another dispute occurred in relation to the Town Wardens, two sets having being appointed to the office; and owing to the undefined *status* of the person who is to be considered an "inhabitant," elections have been shared in by persons of various sorts and conditions—poor men and labourers out of the fields, and itinerants temporarily residing in the place, having given their votes on questions of public importance, by the intervention of interested parties, and thus outnumbered the really qualified residents of the place in their decisions on local affairs. A few years ago (1862) six trustees were living; but they did not attend any meetings, or take part in the management of the property, knowing they would be overwhelmed by the unwarrantable interference of interlopers.

In this state the local government remains at present. The inhabitants—without any specification as to age, sex, or period of inhabitancy—in an annual meeting elect Town Wardens, and have at their disposal the £800 of yearly revenue; though the distribution of the latter is virtually settled by tacit consent among the leading persons of the town. Still, the system exists as described and with all its disadvantages and irregularities in practical working.

The case of Hinckley, which is situated on the south-western side of the County of Leicester, on the border of Warwickshire, differs in some respects from that of Melton Mowbray. It presents peculiarities worthy of distinctive mention, and they will appear in the following historical summary.

At the Norman Conquest, when the defeat of the native English by the Norman conquerors was followed by a complete change of proprietors, the land at Hinckley fell into the possession of Aubrey de Vere, the Lord High Chamberlain of King William.

At this time (about the year 1086) the lordship consisted of fourteen ploughlands, which in the reign of Edward the Confessor—thirty years or so before—had been valued at six pounds' weight of silver, but which now were worth in yearly rent ten pounds' weight, or between thirty and forty pounds in modern reckoning. Earl Aubrey had four ploughs and eight serfs or bondsmen; while forty-two villans (whom, in rural phraseology we may call "smock-frock farmers"), with sixteen bordars or cottagers, and three persons in higher rank and more independent position, called "sokemen," had nine ploughs and a·half. There were, at an extreme computation, supposing every ploughland to consist of 120 acres, 1680 acres under cultivation about Hinckley. From these particulars (still preserved in the Doomsday Survey) it may be inferred that Earl Aubrey kept in his own hands as much as could be ploughed by four ploughs and eight serfs, while the remainder of the inhabitants, all in a more or less dependent condition, worked as much as nine ploughs, and half as much as one plough more, would enable them to do —that is, they had not enough to require ten ploughs to be going regularly. The whole male adult population, all husbandmen, numbered 69.

The Lord of Hinckley succeeding Earl Aubrey was Hugh de Grantmesnil, who was the largest landholder in Leicestershire. He was a Norman and an intimate associate of the Conqueror, and became High Steward of England, as well as possessor of the manor and bailiwick of Hinckley. To him is attributed the erection of the Castle, the formation of a park around it, and the building of the parish church.

The town standing on a sloping site, the spot selected for the Castle was at its upper end, some distance from the dwellings, and there a mound of considerable elevation was raised by the labour of the Earl's serfs and tenants. A deep ditch was dug around it, and on its summit a tower of stone in all probability was erected. In this the armed retainers of the baron were lodged, and by their power the surrounding country was kept in subjection.

With enemies on all sides, composed of the inhabitants dispossessed by the Normans of their lands and homesteads and houses, the soldiers of the Castle needed a stronghold to fly to, and from which they might defy the menaces of the exasperated population.

In this unsettled state of things, the relations of the people of Hinckley to their foreign masters were necessarily hostile. No feelings but one of a determination to rule on one side and to resist on the other, would possibly exist between them; and such must have prevailed during the life-time of Hugh de Grantmesnil. From him to the Earls of Leicester passed the manor and bailiwick of Hinckley. Under these personages, who flourished during the twelfth century, in the successive reigns of William Rufus, Henry the First and Second, Stephen, Matilda, Richard Cœur de Lion, and John, there was a gradual change from the implacable enmity existing shortly after the Conquest to more amicable relationships; as may be inferred from the progress of events in Leicester, where the Earls, during the same epoch, granted charters to the burgesses, guaranteeing to them a restoration of the ancient liberties and customs of which the Conquest had deprived their forefathers.

No charter, however, is extant relative to Hinckley. Doubtless the Earls of Leicester, as its feudal barons, held their Court Leet, at which the inhabitants of the place were bound to do homage and service. This was presided over by a bailiff, who was appointed by the Earl for the time being, and who it was very likely lived at the Castle as the *locum tenens* of his masters, and as the officer in command of its garrison.

The nature and operation of the Court Leet having been already fully explained,[*] need not here be referred to in detail; but may be remembered in connexion with the

[*] See pages 11 and 12.

ensuing narrative. Early in the fifteenth century, Hinckley
began to be designated a "borough." In the year 1416 it
was so called in a book of fifteenths and tenths granted by
the country to Henry the Fourth. The only way of accounting for the use of the term in regard to the place, which
occurs to the writer, is that suggested by the change in the
local ownership. The manor had descended to John of
Gaunt, Duke of Lancaster, whose son, Henry, ascended the
throne as Henry the Fourth. Contemporary with this event,
was the non-residence of the Lancaster family in the Castle
at Leicester, and the consequent severance of their connection with Hinckley, another of their fortified residences. It
is presumed that this would be the period when the inhabitants acquired a certain degree of independence of the
feudal relationship—when they in their Court Leet managed
to a certain extent their own affairs, after paying a
composition to the lords of the manor, and hence the application of the term "borough" to Hinckley commenced.
Having thus acquired the reputation or *status* of a "borough,"
it does not seem to have ever lost it afterwards. It was
recognized, in fact, in public documents; as in 1444, when
Henry the Sixth, in his marriage settlement upon his
intended consort, gave to her the manor of Hinckley,
the borough of Hinckley, and the bond of Hinckley; which
means, we may suppose, that the king gave the rents due
from the lordship, and the fees and payments received on
account of the Court Leet of the borough and the bond, to
the queen, for her use and benefit.

The arrangement between the lords of the manor and the
inhabitants may of course have been revised and suspended
from time to time, and thus the dependency of the latter
on the representatives of the ancient lords been resumed, on
the expiration of contracts made between the two parties;
and besides which, the suppression of the powers of the

Court Leet, by the enactment of laws in the legislature conferring on other tribunals some portion of the ancient authority, entirely altered the aspect of local institutions.

Descending to later times, the Court Leet lost its substantial character, and became a kind of shadow of its former self. In a document dated 1744, it is thus described: "Manor of Hinckley, with the members. To wit, the Court View of Frankpledge and Court Baron of · · · the Lords of the said Manor." A list of names of the Borough Jury "for our sovereign lord the king, as well as for the Lords of the said Manor" follows. In the record, numerous defaulters are stated to have been fined for non-attendance, and constables and third-boroughs chosen. Then comes a long list of penalties levied by the "Borough Jury," for committing small offences; for neglecting to keep pumps and chimneys in repair, for obstructing the roads, for allowing heaps of refuse to accumulate, for using false weights and measures, and so forth. The Bond End Jury seemed to have exercised a wider jurisdiction. Altogether there were thirty-eight laws, principally relating to the town field and to turning-in, numbered in succession—defining the rights of each commoner. The Foreign Jury made regulations for the Castle End of a similar nature to those made for the Borough.

As in the case of Melton Mowbray, there is also a Town Property at Hinckley. It is constituted of two Feoffments, the Greater and the Lesser, the nature of which may be summarised. Some obscurity rests still upon their origin; but, if the example of Melton Mowbray may be allowed to serve for our guidance in the enquiry, the Town Property of Hinckley will be believed to have been transferred from a religious house, fraternity, or chantry, existing before the Reformation, to Feoffees for the use of the inhabitants in secular matters.

Between the date of the Reformation and the reign of James the First, however, abuses in the administration had occurred, leading to an enquiry, which was conducted by commissioners appointed under a commission of charitable uses bearing date the 17th of June, 1603. In October of that year the commissioners made a decree at Leicester, wherein the whole subject was stated and explained. Calling before them witnesses, and examining documents of antiquity, they discovered that "the feoffees thereto had broken the trust committed unto them, and that sundry of the said messuages, burgages, and lands of the best value were mis-governed, under-rented, and long leases made thereof at small rents, *without any valuable consideration given to the benefit of the said town of Hinckley*, contrary to the first intention and mind of the first givers thereof." The commissioners, in proof of their averments, referred to the case of the feoffees of the year 1543 (34th of Henry VIII.) who (four of the seven feoffees being of the same name and near relations) had demised to one of their number, for ninety-nine years, at a rent of one-fifteenth of its yearly value, certain lands and messuages; and to the proceedings of seven other townsmen, tenants of the town property, who were holding their houses at a rent much below the yearly value. By way of remedying the evils thus discovered, the commissioners decreed that the persons profitting by the arrangements above described should renounce their interest and pretended rights, to the new body of feoffees then existing; and that the revenue derived from the property (as Hinckley was "a poor market town," and contained "many poor inhabitants" who had great need of relief) should be applied to meeting the charges and business "imposed and happening" to the inhabitants. With a view to this purpose, the commissioners authorised the feoffees to resume the property, demised and let as already stated, and to re-let and demise it afresh on terms which might be considered just to the interests of the townspeople; the leases not to extend beyond twenty-one years, and the full yearly value to be received. The feoffees were to have the "collection, disposition, and government of the said lands, rents, and tenements yearly," and were required yearly to give an account of them to the Town Masters, on the feast day of St. Thomas, in the Town Hall openly, to which meeting "any other of the inhabitants" were entitled "to resort." A certain portion of the property had, from time immemorial, been employed in the reparation of the parish church, and that appropriation was continued.

The Lesser Feoffment consisted of messuages, houses, and so forth, held under a separate trust; but the proceeds from which were applied in a similar way to those derived from the property described as the Greater Feoffment. Yearly accounts were to be presented in the manner before specified.

In addition to the two Feoffments, the Manor trust has to be briefly described. All that remained in the reign of James the First of the property, authority, and rights of seigniory of the former lords of the place consisted in about seventy acres of land, with the right to summon the inhabitants to the Court Leet and to levy fines for non-attendance. These were conveyed to four feoffees by the direction and appointment of Charles, Earl of Nottingham. In the year 1793, the feoffees of the town sold the land to the farmers by whom it was occupied; the only remaining property being three small tenements, and certain cottages erected on the waste of the manor, with the usual manorial claim to waifs, and so forth. At the present day, the Court Leets are summoned, and transact the same kind of business as that mentioned in the document dated 1744. The power which in ancient days the lord of the manor, by his steward, assisted by a jury, probably exercised—of condemning offenders against the law to the gallows, the pillory, the cuckstool, and the stocks, and of casting into prison the insolvent debtor, or the obdurate suitor of the court—has dwindled down to a yearly dinner, and to what resembles a grotesque formality rather than a public ceremony. A jury is sworn, which has has no causes to try, and a mimic Mayor (really the chief bailiff) is appointed, who is denuded of authority.

In the County History* these statements are made respecting the town:—

"Under its original lords, the town of Hinckley enjoyed the privileges of a Borough; and, from their connexion with the *Lancaster* family, the inhabitants took a decided part in the civil contests. But, whatever their privileges were, they became forfeited to the conquering monarch of the house of *York*. The lordship, however, is still divided into two distinct liberties, the Borough and the Bond; and the former of which divisions has its peculiar privileges. · · The whole number of town officers are fifteen, namely, chosen at the Court Leet; for the Borough, the Mayor or Bailiff, one constable, two head-boroughs; for the Bond, one constable, three head-boroughs. The Mayor of Hinckley, who must necessarily be an inhabitant, residing within the Borough, has authority to regulate the markets and examine the weights. · · · The Borough, as far as I can find, is the only part of the ancient property from which a chief rent is reserved to the Crown in right of the Duchy of Lancaster."

The statement of the forfeiture of ancient privileges rests solely on the authority of the History, which does not refer

* *Nichols's History of the County of Leicester:* Sparkenhoe Hundred.

to any documentary evidence in support of it. Owing to the entire absence of local charters and manuscripts of a date before the sixteenth century, there are no means of ascertaining what the actual state of affairs was which constituted the place a borough—whether there was an officer placed on the footing of a Mayor—or whether an organization existed which could by any stretch of definition be properly designated a Corporation. There can be no doubt that the grim symbol of the law's power, the gallows, formerly stood close to the town ; a pillory was also standing in the Borough ; and an ancient Town Hall occupied a site in its very centre. The former Earls of Leicester also, in right of their honour of Hinckley, bore a distinctive banner, which, in heraldic phraseology, was "*party per pale, indented, argent, and gules.*" All these things—the gallows, the pillory, the Town Hall, the distinctive banner—indicate a Past in which the community here resident had a corporate unity, and a position among the old centres of English population.

An example of local administration, long continued and distinctly recognised, is supplied by the town of Loughborough. On the high road of railway communication, between the North and South of England, as it passes through the Midlands, scarcely an English traveller can fail to have noticed the fine tower of the parish church, with the hills of Charnwood Forest in the back-ground, and the low meadows around. It was in this district, before the drainage of the land by the cultivators of the soil had prevented the excessive accumulation of the rainfalls, and the flowing of the water from the woodland slopes into the lower ground, that a large pool or lake would appear to have been in existence. Near its banks an Anglo-Saxon settlement was formed. From the names given to it, we may learn that the primitive dwellers on the site knew it either as the "lake-stream," or the "lake-fortification"—the terms "Lochteburne," and "Luchleburne," being employed to designate it in the Doomsday Survey by the Norman copyists, and "Lughteburgh" being also another ancient appellation, which in modern times is pronounced "Luffburrow." The chief proprietor at the time of the Conquest was Hugh de Grantmesnil, under whom five or six principal tenants occupied portions of the soil. In the thirteenth century the de Spencers, in the fourteenth the de Beaumonts, in the fifteenth the Hastingses were lords of the manor, which was always one of considerable size and importance; the term "borough," or "bury" implying (according to certain authorities) the chief residence of a manorial lord—Loughborough having been regarded as a royal village in the time of the Saxons, though it was never a town corporate. During the whole period of its history the inhabitants were amenable to the regulations of its Court Leet, which was held annually in the month of December. At this court, presided over by the steward of the lord of the manor, a jury of twelve men were chosen, whose functions had dwindled down, at the close of the last century, to the prevention of encroachments in building, planting, and so forth, and to deciding and settling various kinds of controversies and differences in the parish concerning property, nuisances, and similar matters. Two constables, two third-boroughs, street-masters, field-reeves, and pinders, were also elected by the court; whose business was transacted in an ancient building called the "Court Leet Chamber." Adjacent to this was a small prison—a relic of the times when the powers of the Court were more extensive; and a whipping post also stood in the town. In addition to this, there was "the Old Gaol," another place of confinement for criminals.

A very considerable estate was conveyed to this town by one of the inhabitants—Thomas Burton, a merchant of the staple of Calais, in the reign of Henry the Seventh; but whether it had been previously his own property, or the property of a religious fraternity, no records extant bear witness. The lands and tenements thus given lay in the town and adjacent villages. In a deed appointing new eoffees, dated 1597, the purposes for which the rents and profits were to be applied were defined to be these—the relief of the poor people of Loughborough; the making and repairing fifty arches of the bridges in and about the town; the maintenance of a free grammar school, and the payment of public taxes and common charges. A bridge-master was to be chosen yearly by the honest and substantial men of the place, who was empowered to collect the rents and apply the proceeds as he should think proper.

From what has been said relative to the situation of Loughborough, the necessity of such an extensive number of arches to carry roads over the low, damp meadows, will have become apparent; and the existence of the Bridge-master as the principal local officer is thus accounted for. At Melton Mowbray, we have seen, the Town Wardens occupied a corresponding position. But at Loughborough, though the concluding syllables of the name would seem to indicate the existence of an independent town-community, none such was ever known. There are certain features in common possessed by these places. Each had its town estate, the income of which was applied to the maintenance of a school after the Reformation, to the making and repair of roads, to the relief of the poor, to the liquidation of the public imposts, and so forth. In Hinckley and Loughborough, it has been shown, the Court Leet exercised its jurisdiction; as it did doubtless at Melton Mowbray; the history of the institution in each town being modified by local circumstances.

CHAPTER XIV.

ON TOWNS UNINCORPORATED—CONCLUDED.

Manchester—now the second city in the British Empire—is an example of a large town existing unincorporated until a late period, though possessing in the middle ages a certain degree of local independence. The problem it offers to the student of municipal history is, therefore, at once interesting and suggestive, and entitled to consideration in an essay like the present.

In the Roman period, the place was known by two names—Mancunium and Mamucium—one of which may have been a mis-spelling of the other. A Roman *Castrum*, superior in size and importance to the majority of those established in the island, was formed here, and connected by the military roads with other parts of the country. It was in all probability garrisoned by a cohort of Frisians, attached to the Twentieth Legion stationed at Chester. There was, therefore, a purely Teutonic population located here before the Saxon invasion. In the seventh century (689) the town was known as Mamecestre; an old Welsh Chronicle recording the presence here of queen Ethelberga and Ina, king of Wessex, at that period. About a century and a half before the Norman Conquest, Mamecestre was rebuilt and re-fortified by the orders of king Edward (923). The town had, however, no position as a borough when the Doomsday Survey was compiled; its inhabitants being then under the Sheriff's authority, and within the jurisdiction of the hundred of Salford. Two churches were standing on the site; indicating the settlement of a more numerous population there than was usual in a mere village or hamlet. But History seems to have passed them by, unobservant, until the agents of the Conqueror visited the spot, to see what they could enter into their catalogue of the locality.

The first Norman lord of the soil was Albert Grelle, or Gresley, who held under Roger de Poictou, as baron of Mamecestre, probably between the years 1086 and 1100, and who was the predecessor of a long line of descendants. They held a Court Baron in their manor of Manchester, which comprised several "vills," called its members, with their hamlets, and a large number of freehold tenants; but the position held by the manor was secondary to the honour. The fifth of the line of Norman barons of Mamecestre was Robert Gresley, who lived in the place—it is supposed in a residence on the ground known as the Baron's "hull" or hill, and who obtained a charter for a yearly fair in the town. But it was not until the time of the eighth baron, Thomas, that it rose above the condition of a mere village to that of an independently-governed community or "borough," and that its inhabitants were designated "burgesses."

This took place in the year 1301, when Thomas Greslet or Gresley granted a charter to the inhabitants, which by withdrawing them in part from the jurisdiction of the county authorities, and placing them under their own local officers, imparted to them a separate town-individuality. Seventy years before, the people of the closely adjoining borough of Salford had received a charter from their lord, Randle Blundeville, Earl of Chester, whereby they were endowed with the privileges necessary to the maintenance and enjoyment of local freedom, and placed in a position to be envied by their neighbours across the Irwell. "It is probable," as the historian[*] suggests, "that the better government

---

[*] *Mamecestre*, vol. 2, by John Harland, Esq., F.S.A.; Chetham Society publications.

of Salford, and the greater privileges enjoyed by its
inhabitants, may have caused sufficient pressure to be
applied to the lord of the manor of Mamecestre, to extort,
or perhaps to purchase, the Charter from him. It is clear
that the unprivileged dweller in Mamecestre had only to
give up his dwelling there and cross the Irwell, to place
himself at once in a much better social position ; and it is
not unreasonable to suppose that, if no other argument
were sufficiently cogent, that of numerous vacated burgages
might awaken Thomas Grelle to the necessity of offering
some chartered inducements to his tenants to remain in
Mamecestre."

On turning to the Charter itself* we ascertain what the
inhabitants of Mamecestre regarded as the essentials of
local freedom at the very commencement of the fourteenth
century. To become a burgess, an inhabitant was required
to hold in the place a portion of land and a house—called
a "burgage." In Salford the area of the "burgage" was
an acre, and the same extent probably was allotted to a
burgess in Mamecestre. For this plot, the tenant paid 12d.
yearly to the lord of the manor in lieu of all service; and
he might bequeath it and his chattels, if he had no heir, to
whomsoever he pleased, saving the services due to the
baron. In case of leaving a widow, she might live in the
house, and the heir with her ; but on re-marrying she was
to depart, leaving the heir in possession. If a burgess
wished to sell his burgage he might do so, on giving to the
lord fourpence, and he might then go freely whithersoever
he desired. On the death of a burgess, his heir was to
give no other "relief" to a lord except arms of some kind;
perhaps those he used during life—for every burgess then
kept weapons, being either an archer or a pikeman, having
also a sword.

* See *Mamecestre*, vol. 2, p. 218 : Chetham Society publications.

Among the advantages of being a burgess in Mamecestre, after having acquired a settled residence, in case of any dispute with a fellow-burgess, or of sustaining personal injury, was the obtaining of justice on the spot—that is, in the local court called the " Portmanmote." One of the clauses of the Charter expressly says:

> "Also if any one shall be impleaded in the borough of
> "any plea, he need not make answer either to bur-
> "gess or villein, *save in his Portmanmote*, not even to
> "a vavasour [that is, an inferior lord holding his lands
> "in subjection to a superior lord], except to a plea
> "that belongeth to the king's crown, and in one for
> "robbery [or theft.]"

Under the operation of this clause, the burgesses were protected against the law-proceedings in courts without the borough, especially in the sheriff's tourn, or itinerating court; in all matters, in fact, except those over which the Crown had jurisdiction, and charges of larceny, of which the lord of the manor took cognizance. In case one burgess wounded another on the Lord's day—between noon (or three o'clock) on Saturday and Monday being the time thus designated—he was liable to a fine of 20s. If one burgess struck another, without drawing blood, and succeeded in returning to his house without being arrested by the reeve, he escaped forfeiture. The reeve was required to bind a townsman over, by his own recognizance and the sureties of bondsmen, to appear in court, and answer a charge of wounding another, were the offender taken outside his house.

The Portmanmote (which was really synonymous with the Court Leet*) was the tribunal to which the burgesses had recourse in all matters besides, and was held before the lord

---

* See *Manchester Court Leet Records*, p. 15, by John Harland, Esq., F.S.A.: Chetham Society publications.

of the manor's steward. There was a Lagh-mote, a smaller Portmote, held by adjournment between the quarterly Portmotes; but not a distinct institution. By this court, cases of debt were decided; and the burgesses might arrest any debtor—knight, priest, or clerk—who might be found in the borough, and bring him before the Portmanmote. No doubt, also, the usage was to make transfers of property before the same body. Besides the facility of obtaining justice in a local court, the burgess was exempt from the payment of tolls within the fee of the lord of the manor; while non-residents were bound to pay them. In those simple times, too, when every townsman probably kept pigs, the burgesses were permitted to fatten the same in the woods of their baron.

A most important right was that vested in the burgesses of choosing their own "reeve":

"Also, the burgesses ought, and have power, to choose
"the reeve, of themselves, whom they will, and to
"remove the reeve."

This officer is called in the Latin *præfectus villæ*. In the case of Preston, it has been stated* that the term was equivalent to the word mayor; the latter being of later use and Norman derivation. There were no "pretors" or bailiffs in Mamecestre, as at Preston; and therefore the reeve had a greater number of duties to fulfil at the former place than the latter. He seems to have instituted pleas, to have interfered between creditor and debtor, to have officiated in the arrest of a quarrelsome burgess, to have apprehended thieves, to have been present at all sales and bargains, to have given possession of shops and sheds to burgesses and renters of such places, and to have received the lord's-rents and other payments due to him.† He had assistants, not

---

* See *ante* page 99.

† See *Mamecestre*; vol. 2, pp. 218 to 237.

specially designated. As truly remarked by the editor of the book whence these particulars are compiled, "The power granted by this clause in the Mamecestre Charter [that last quoted] for the burgesses to choose and to remove their own reeve, was a great safeguard of their feudal liberties; because they could always avoid electing a creature of the lord of the manor, and on the contrary could secure as their chief officer and ruler one who would assert their rights as against the lord, his steward, and his bailiffs in the courts and elsewhere."

The lord of the manor received the various penalties paid by offending and defaulting burgesses; and the inhabitants were obliged to grind their corn at his mill and to bake their bread in his bakehouse; so that his receipts from these various sources must have been considerable.

In Mamecestre no Merchant Guild existed; not the remotest allusion being made to such a body in the charter of Thomas Gresley, its feudal lord. From one of the clauses, it appears that "merchants" had shops or sheds in the places and that they paid a certain amount therefore as strangers; burgesses also having shops or sheds in the Market-place, on account of which they paid a smaller sum. There was clearly a distinction of class between the merchants and the burgesses, implied in the use of the terms as distinctive of each body; and the former were apparently non-resident. Had a Guild been in operation in Mamecestre, the resident burgesses would have been its members: they would have taken an oath of mutual fidelity, would have elected their Mayor and Council and other officers, would have regulated the commercial and general affairs of the place, would have had a common purse, would have levied payments, would have passed laws for their own internal management—would, in short, have constituted a corporation in all except certain legal senses, before explained and defined. But to this *status* they never attained. Indeed, though the inhabitants were called "burgesses" in their charter—from which it may be presumed that they were held to be inhabitants of a borough—it appeared, on an injunction being taken at Preston in the year 1359, to determine whether Roger la Warre should hold Mamecestre as a borough, that he was not justified in so doing. The Duke of Lancaster had, it seems, by his bailiffs fined certain residents of the place for violating the regulations respecting bread and ale, and for breaking the peace, and certain butchers for selling contrary to the assize; against which proceedings Roger la Warre appealed, on the ground of the place being a borough, and therefore exempt from the Duke's jurisdiction; but in vain—as the inquisitors decided that Roger la Warre did not hold the town of Mamecestre as a borough. The inhabitants, therefore, were not correctly speaking "burgesses." Had they been inhabitants of a town in which a Guild Merchant had been established —as Lancaster, Preston, Liverpool, and Wigan were—they might have been so designated; but not strictly and properly otherwise. The result of the inquisition was to re-institute the jurisdiction of the wapentake of Salford and that of the Sheriff's tourn within the town of Mamecestre, "in all cases except such as related to the lord and his tenants, which, according to the ancient usage, would be determinable by the Court Baron."*

For more than five centuries, the townspeople of Manchester lived under the authority of their Court. Its records (in the language of their able and painstaking expositor†) show

"How the people of this little town were ruled; what
" power was vested in their governors; how they lived,

* *Mamecestre*, vol. 3, pp. 450 to 460.

† *Manchester Court Leet Records*, vol. 639. The Chetham Society publications: Introduction.

"ate and drank, bought and sold, built and pulled
"down; how they were supplied with wheat and corn,
"fruit and vegetables, bread and water and ale; with
"flesh meat and poultry; with cloth and leather, hats
"and caps, boots and shoes; how tradesmen had their
"businesses shackled by strange and foolish restric-
"tions; how those who made or sold bad articles were
"dealt with; how bakers and alesellers were regulated
"by 'the Assise of Bread and Ale,' and punished by
"fines, by stocks and pillory; how rigidly all the
"manipulators in leather, tanners, tawers and dressers,
"curriers and shoemakers, were liable to penalties for
"gashing and otherwise maltreating hides and skins, or
"for one following not only his own branch of trade,
"but that of another, or for dealing with leather not
"stamped or sealed by the official sealer; how butter
"or even suet was prohibited in bread or cakes for sale,
"and wedding dinners at public houses were limited to a
"cost of fourpence per head; how every burgess and
"other inhabitant was bound to do suit and service, by
"attendance at least, at the Leet Court, and every in-
"habitant required to sweep before his door, and to
"repair the street from his frontage to the crown of
"the road, to grind at the lord's mill and bake at the
"lord's oven; and how all had to get their water from
"the Conduit in regular 'cale' or turn."

The writer thus continues:—

"Nothing scarcely was too large, certainly nothing too
"small, for presentment to and adjudication by the
"Court Leet jury. An Earl of Derby presided person-
"ally in this court as the steward of the lord of the
"manor; and a whole regiment of manorial officers
"were present, from the clerk of the court, the borough-
"reeve and constables, the catchpoll, the lord's bailiff,

"the bylawmen, and the market-lookers of fish and
"flesh and white meats, down to the ale-conners,
"scavengers, dog-muzzlers, pinder and swineherd.
"Amongst the local institutions may be named the
"waits or town minstrels, the fountain and conduit,
"the booths, (apparently sessions and court house and
"market hall); the archery butts, the cockpit, the
"pound or pinfold, the lord's mill and his bakehouse,
"the gallows and pillory, the stocks, the whipping-post,
"tumbrel, brank or bridle for scolds, and the ducking-
"stool and pond for disorderly women. * * * Then
"there was the legislation for and about animals.
"Cows, horses, sheep, pigs, dogs,—all required regula-
"tion, and had it. Pigs, as the most perverse animals,
"required the firmest and most rigorous handling; and
"hundreds of folio pages of jury orders relate to 'swine'
"alone, and their numerous misdeeds and nuisances,
"their eating corn in the market, and desecrating the
"church yard. Amongst the heaviest fines, or as they
"were called 'amercements,' on the butchers, were those
"for selling bull-beef, the bull not having been previ-
"ously baited to make the flesh tender enough for
"human food. * * * Swords and other
"weapons are forbidden to be worn, and none but
"worshipful and right worshipful persons are allowed
"to wear hats; cap-makers being appointed to go to
"church to note all delinquents. Waits are to 'do
"their duty and use themselves honestly as honest men
"owe to do.' Watchmen are to be 'honest, discreet,
"and sober men, being able to yield account of their
"living favourites to virtue and enemies to vice.' No
"man is to take a lodger, unless satisfied he can earn
"his living without begging."

In the condition of a market-town did Manchester remain until the year 1838, when it was incorporated by royal charter; its title as a city dating from the year 1853. Such is the simple story of the municipal development of a town which "has now become the greatest manufacturing place in the world; the centre and capital of the largest spinning and weaving works known in the annals of civilization."

CHAPTER XV.

MUNICIPAL INSIGNIA.

In the ancient towns of England, when under the sway of the Romans, the usages of municipal life were doubtless similar to those practised throughout the empire. It may be assumed that the chief officers of each city or station were ordinarily attended by subordinate functionaries, as they were in Rome itself. The Prætors or Consuls, as they walked along the streets, were preceded by their sergeants or beadles, designated Lictors, who carried in their hands a number of rods, with one or two axes surmounting the whole, which were fastened in bundles, and were capable of being separated, to be used for scourging or beheading criminals. The *fasces*, in consequence of their invariable association with the magistrates, became regarded as the emblems of justice; and the spear was regarded as a sign of authority, that weapon being set up in the forum or market-place, when the Decemviri, chosen by the Prætor to judge of such matters as he deemed them competent to determine, discharged their functions. The spear was also exhibited at the collection of the taxes by the Censors. Whether the use of the *fasces* and the spear survived the presence of the Roman officials in this country is a question left in some obscurity; but in France, owing to the continuity of the municipal system, and the unbroken succession of races in the occupation of some parts of the country, it seems probable that the ancient emblems of civic power and justice never fell into disuse.

In Amiens, the insignia of supreme justice, implying the possession of the right of life and death over the citizens, continued to accompany the mayor and aldermen on all public occasions, long after their ancient authority had departed.* These attributes of their lost power consisted of two swords of antique shape, carried in the hands of two officials, called, in reference to their employment, "espadrons." A similar custom formerly prevailed among almost all the great corporations of France. In Toulouse, the large sabre is still preserved which formerly served its magistrates as the equivalent of the Consular axes. It is a scimitar, sloping towards the point, without a guard, and a weapon of imposing appearance.

The use of the sword, as an emblem of municipal authority, or of the *fasces*, is not traceable in this country before the Norman Conquest; and, indeed, it is doubtful whether an object of any kind or shape was employed in the way here described, until the example was set by the metropolis in the fourteenth century. The most ancient and generally-used ensign of authority was the mace, which was originally an implement of war, invented for the purpose of breaking through the steel helmets or armour of the cavalry of the middle ages. It was borne by the chief magistrates of boroughs as a weapon; sometimes at the head of the townsmen called forth to battle, at others to strike down the rebellious townsmen in civil turmoils. As the esquire of the knight carried his lance, when not engaged in combat, so the sergeant of the Mayor bore the mace before his master. We learn that it was not until toward the close of the reign of Edward the Third [1366-1377, A.D.] that the sergeants of the city of London were empowered by royal charter to carry maces of gold or silver, or plated with silver, and ornamented with the royal arms.†

A sword was borne before the city authorities in ancient times. In the city of Lincoln, when Richard the Second visited it in the year 1386, he granted to the Mayor and his

---

* Thierry's *Lettres sur l'Histoire de France*, 2nd ed., p. 388.

† *Liber Albus* (already quoted) page 137.

successors the privilege of having a sword carried before them in their processions. Following the example of London, twenty years after its first use of the mace as a municipal emblem, it may have been adopted in direct imitation of the citizens of the metropolis.

Thirty or forty years after the date of the London charter, the citizens of Norwich, emulous of the example of the metropolis, fancied their importance was incomplete until they too, possessed an emblem of their dignity. Next in size and populousness to London, Norwich then aspired to be on an equality, in regard to external pretensions, with her more distinguished sister. Having (as before stated) favoured the pretensions of Henry, Duke of Lancaster (son of John of Gaunt), they were presented by him with a sword, which, on his ascending the throne, he permitted the mayor and sheriffs to have carried before them with the point erect, in the presence of all lords or nobles of the realm, whether they were of the blood royal or not—excepting only in his own presence and that of his heirs. At the same time, the sergeants of the mayor and sheriffs were to carry gold or silver maces, gilt or ungilt, with the king's arms thereon, both in the king's presence and in that of the queen consort or queen mother, in the city and its county, as their proper sergeants-at-arms. The carrying of the sword before the city magnates was also copied from the example of London; as that city had apparently derived the custom from the great French municipalities.

How the custom extended, it is not intended here minutely to describe; but one or two other instances of its adoption may be cited.

At Exeter, Henry the Seventh, on the occurrence of some dissensions among the Mayor and Common Councilmen, relative to the choice of the Mayor and other officers [1497, A.D.], summoned them before him, and directed another method of election to be pursued in future. The king nominated as the first Mayor under the new order of things a person who had formerly been one of his servants, and who had been a bailiff of the city. Taking the sword from his own side, Henry gave it to the newly-made Mayor, with a cap of maintenance, to encourage him to persevere in his duty; the sword to be carried in state before the Mayor and his successors for ever, as was the usage in the city of London.

At the city of Canterbury, by virtue of a charter granted by Henry VI., sergeants-at-mace were appointed by the Mayor, and they carried the emblem before him on public occasions. In the Burghmote Rolls an event is recorded in connection with the usage, showing the importance attached to the custom. It is this:—Queen Mary had been staying at Canterbury, and was proceeding thence through the suburb of Wincheap, to Eastwell, on a visit to Sir Thomas Moyle. Before her majesty rode the Mayor, mace in hand, till he came to a certain point, where he was met by Sir Thomas Moyle, then the High Sheriff, who required the Mayor to lay down the mace; but the latter refused to do so, saying he would bear the mace as far as the liberty of the city went. He did so; the Sheriff giving place to him thus far, and bearing no rod of office. At the point of the boundary, the Mayor took leave of the Queen, who gave him her most hearty thanks.—The Mayor felt that within the city boundaries he was supreme in office, the Sheriff having no jurisdiction therein; and therefore he insisted on the precedence which he maintained.*

In the borough of Leicester, maces of silver and copper were in use in the year 1517 (how much earlier is unknown), and were carried before the Mayor by his sergeants on public occasions. In the reign of Edward the Sixth, a great mace

* *Notes and Queries*, Second Series, vol. 5, p. 270.

and four small maces were entrusted to the Mayor, to be held by his successors in succession, with other valuable articles for municipal use. A circumstance which affords a striking idea of the importance attached to the mace as a municipal symbol took place in the year 1766. It may be here introduced:—

In accordance with ancient usage, every year, on the Monday after Martinmas-day (November 11), the newly-elected Mayor, preceded by the mace-bearer, walked to the great hall of the Castle, there to take an oath before the Steward of the Duchy of Lancaster that he would well and faithfully respect every ancient custom, jurisdiction, privilege, and pre-eminence of the Duchy, within the borough of Leicester, being a part of that Duchy. The ancient earldom of Leicester having been vested through descent in the earldom, and subsequently dukedom, of Lancaster; and the latter having merged in the sovereign authority, on the accession of Henry, duke of Lancaster, to the throne as Henry the Fourth; the homage due to the ancient feudal lords of Leicester was thereafter required to be paid to the kings of England, or their steward, as representatives of the former local barons. When the Mayor reached the gateway, through which admission was obtained to the yard of the Castle, the mace-bearer always lowered the mace, in token of submission to the power which had formerly ruled the Borough, and its modern representatives. But in the year above named, the mace-bearer purposely neglected to "slope the mace," and the Constable of the Castle refused him admission in consequence. An angry controversy was the result. The real occasion of this violation of ancient custom is supposed to have been the fact of the Mayor being a partizan of the exiled Stuarts; and, six years after George the Third was on the throne, venturing in this covert way to disown his legitimacy.

Y

In Preston, the local authorities were not authorized to exhibit the mace until the Charter of Queen Elizabeth, granted in 1565, empowered them to do so. But here another custom of kindred nature exists: the Mayor and members of the Corporation are preceded, on state occasions, by two officers in livery, each bearing a halberd. These weapons are placed outside the door of the residence of the Mayor for the time being, as insignia of his office. They are by no means indifferent modern representatives of the Roman *fasces* and *secures*, or the bundle of rods with the axe fixed in the centre. The shaft is much decorated, and the brass head exhibits an axe as well as a spear.

All these insignia—the mace, the sword, the halberd, and the spear—have been obviously retained in token of the authority which their original use implied. When the rude times passed away, in which the mace was actually employed, an ornamental article superseded it and became symbolic of supreme local authority. In like manner the sword (usually two-handed) was formerly used to behead offenders, and the official before whom it was held had the power to employ it on behalf of the community over whom he presided. He had in his hands the "high justice" of the locality. When, however, the right to decree and execute capital punishment, was taken from city magistrates and entrusted to state functionaries, the sword was still preserved as an emblem of the ancient authority of the city or borough officials.

A sentiment of civic pride was also gratified by the exhibition of the mace and the sword in public processions, in former times, which was cherished by every inhabitant of a city or borough. Its origin was natural. Individually obscure, perhaps, the citizen identified himself with the municipality, the dignity and glory of which he shared, which in its unity and totality he was proud to see equal in rank and authority to any one of the insolent and tyrannical barons of the adjoining districts. Free within the walls of his own city, he was thus consoled for the ignominy of treatment he sometimes experienced outside its limits. When he saw the mace and the sword—when he saw the banner of his community unfurled,—his heart exulted in the thought that his fellow-citizens and he constituted a body enjoying entire independence, their own civil and criminal jurisdiction, and a name in the land which kings and lords respected. It is this tradition of former local freedom and self-government which the antique municipal insignia even yet preserved exemplify, endearing them to those who know their history and appreciate their significance.

CHAPTER XVI.

THE FRENCH COMMUNES.

It will have been perceived, in the course of the foregoing chapters, that indications have been incidentally afforded of the influence of ideas derived from the other side of the British Channel, upon the minds of the people of this country. It has been noticed, for instance, that the term "mayor," in its application to the chief officer of a borough, first used in the metropolis at the close of the reign of John, was introduced from France, having been known at Beauvais a hundred years before. The word "commune," in like manner, occurs in English municipal documents of the thirteenth and fourteenth centuries, and is well known as one of familiar and frequent employment in French protocols of a preceding epoch. So the word "jurats" or "jurrets," in connection with those who constituted the Council of the Guild, was one which was probably borrowed from the French burgesses. This phraseology—this adoption of the words "mayor," "commune," and "jurat", instead of terms of English derivation, as "alderman," "guild," and so forth—betrays a foreign origin, among a people speaking the "Roman" tongue. The supposition renders a brief account of the rise and extension of the French municipalities, and a comparison between them and the English boroughs, in some measure desirable; since we may thus ascertain how far the sympathies of townsmen with each other in the two countries operated in mutual encouragement to extend local freedom, and how the efforts of the more advanced municipalities stimulated the less advanced to imitate their example.

Towards the close of the eleventh century, a number of ancient cities in the south of Gaul had acquired positions of municipal independence, which were owing in great part to their long establishment, and to the continuity of the Roman organization in their limits from the time of the empire to later periods. By degrees, the towns to the north of the Loire aspired to the possession of similar freedom and exemption from external control ; seeking to form what they sometimes called " republics." The enthusaism of the time spread until it produced revolutions in every district where a population was found sufficiently numerous to enter upon a struggle with the feudal power, and the peasants of the surrounding country swelled the number of the insurgent townsmen. The inhabitants of the places which this political movement had reached, assembled in the principal church or in the market place, and there, upon the holy relics, took an oath to support each other, and not to allow any man to do wrong to any one of their number or to treat him as a serf. It was this oath or " conjuration," as ancient documents call it, which gave birth to the " commune." All those who were bound together in this manner took thenceforth the name of " communers" or " jurors," and to them these new titles comprehended ideas of duty, fidelity, and reciprocal devotion, expressed in ancient times by the word " citizen." By way of a guarantee of their association, the members of the commune constituted, at first tumultuously and afterwards in a more regular manner, an elective government, resembling in some respects the municipal government of the Romans, and differing from it in others. Instead of the names of *curia* and *decurion*, which had fallen into disuse, the communes of the south adopted that of *consul*, which recalled grand ideas, and the communes of the north those of "juror" and "echevin;" although the last title, on account of its Teutonic origin, was tainted to them with a remembrance of serfdom. The new magistrates were called on to be constantly at the head of the burgesses in their struggles with their ancient lords, and therefore were empowered to assemble them by the ringing of the public bell, and to lead them under the banner of the commune.

In the south of Gaul, where the ancient Roman towns were the most numerous, and where, the Germanic invasions having had least effect, they had better preserved their population and their riches, the attempts at enfranchisement were, if not more energetic, at least more completely successful. These were the only towns which fully attained to that republican standard which was in some measure the ideal whereto all the communes aspired. In the north, the contest was longer and the success less decisive. A circumstance unfavourable to the towns of the latter region was the double dependence in which they lived, under the power of their lords and the sovereignty of the king of France or the emperor of Germany; for in the midst of a contest against the first of these powers, the second intervened for his own profit, and often occasioned a renewal of the struggle when everything seemed to have been settled; the kings of France declaring for or against the towns, according to the sum of money which one or other of the parties offered for their interference.

In these municipal revolutions, the burgesses of the eleventh and twelfth centuries pushed their desire for reform to its extreme limit. Without any remembrance of Grecian or Roman history—whether their town was under the rule of a king or a baron, or a bishop, or an abbey, they went directly for a republic; but the reaction of established authority very soon threw them into the background. From the balancing of these two opposing forces resulted for the town a kind of mixed government, and this is what happened in the north of France, as the charters of the communes testify.

The principle of the communes of the Middle Ages, the enthusiasm which induced their founders to brave all dangers and all miseries, was indeed that of liberty; but of a liberty quite material—the liberty of going and of coming, of selling and of buying, of being master in one's own house, and of leaving one's property to one's children. In this first need of independence which agitated men, on leaving the chaos wherein the Roman world had, as it were, been swallowed up after the barbarian invasions, it was personal safety, everyday security, the ability of accumulating and keeping, which was the ultimate end of their efforts and their pledges. Human intelligence did not then conceive anything more elevated, anything more desirable in the human condition; and men devoted themselves to obtain, by dint of labour, what, in modern Europe, constitutes our ordinary life, and what the simple policy of modern states assures to all classes of subjects, without any necessity for charters.

Like the constitutions of our own age the communes were erected one after another, and the last in date imitated point after point the organization of the older ones. Thus the commune of Laon organized itself on the model of the communes of St. Quentin and Noyon, and afterwards the charter of Laon served as a pattern for those of Crespy and Montdidier. The charter of Soissons, which appears to have enjoyed the greatest celebrity, is reproduced in the texts of those of Fisme, Senlis, Compèigne, and Sens. This charter was carried into Burgundy; the inhabitants of Dijon renouncing their own ancient municipal system in its favour. At the moment when, in France, the first communal constitution was formed, there was scarcely a town which had not in it the germ of a similar change; but favourable circumstances were necessary to its development. It was above all necessary that the example should be set by some neighbouring town : sometimes it was the report of an insurrection in one which made it break out in others, as a fire spreads itself; sometimes it was the granting of a charter which brought trouble on a province. The revolution of Laon, the bloodiest of all, was occasioned by the establishment of the communes of St. Quentin and Noyon ; the one consented to by a baron, the other instituted by a bishop. The blow struck at Laon made itself immediately felt at Amiens, then at Soissons, then at Rheims. The commune of Noyon, although it had found in some sort a legislator in its bishop, was the daughter of that of Cambray, where that bishop had gained his experience and his political ideas.

The positions of these burgess associations offered a crowd of degrees and shades, from a republican city which, like Toulouse, had kings for its allies, maintained an army, and exercised all the rights of sovereignty, to the collections of serfs and vagabonds to whom kings and lords offered an asylum on their domains ; the latter class being always subject to a bailiff of the king or lord, the charters guaranteeing only to the inhabitants the enjoyment of some civil rights. But they were sufficient to draw travelling workmen, small peddling traders, and peasants, who were serfs, in respect to their body and goods, to fix their habitations on the spot.

The municipalities of the first class in Languedoc, Normandy, Anjou, Brittany, Guyenne, and Provence, were left long undisturbed for state reasons : but they were ultimately undermined, and, so to speak, demolished piece by piece. With regard to the towns of the second and third class, the kings showed great liberality towards them, because they did not fear such would succeed in becoming independent ; and therefore they conceded without trouble to insignificant places a title and constitution which they had obstinately refused to larger towns. When, in consequence of insurrection, and the treaties which rendered it legitimate, the movement of the burgess class towards enfranchisement had become a social impulse, and one of the necessities of the epoch, the powers of the day lent themselves to it with an apparent good grace, all the time having an eye to material advantage without incurring any imminent peril. Thence arose the enormous quantities of seignorial, and above all, royal charters, conceded during the thirteenth century.

These institutions, so full of interest in their origin and growth, and obtained by severe and sanguinary struggles, did not, however, endure long: they were all destroyed, one after another, by royal proclamations, between the fourteenth and seventeenth centuries, and the entire local authority was then vested in the bailiffs appointed by the sovereigns in succession. Nor have the ancient cities of France been able again to raise themselves, in later ages, to their former semi-republican condition.*

---

*See *Lettres sur l'Histoire de France*, par Aug. Thierry: lettre 13, "Sur l'Affranchissement des Communes."

CHAPTER XVII.

A COMPARISON BETWEEN THE FRENCH COMMUNES AND ENGLISH BOROUGHS.

In the foregoing summary of the rise and fall of the communes of France, some points of difference and others of resemblance between the English and French municipalities, will have been suggested.

In regard to the origin of the French communes it will have been seen, for example, that in the South of France the connection between the later Roman municipal organization and the medieval system was probably never broken, and that the cities of the North imitated the institutions of the South to a great extent, modifying their administration in accordance with the necessities of their position. We are prepared, therefore, to find a more strict family likeness between the more modern and the more ancient forms of city government in France than in England, where, between the middle of the fifth and the middle of the seventh centuries, a kind of anarchy and utter lawlessness prevailed; the towns being sometimes depopulated and destroyed (as in the case of St. Albans), and the transmission of the traditions of Roman rule entirely stopped in consequence. France has indeed always, in every stage of its history, evidenced the deep impress of classical ideas upon its national character and institutions; while England has, on the contrary, in its language and the nature of its institutions, shown how much it has derived from the spirit and manners of the Germanic races by whom it was originally so largely peopled.

The events of history have also greatly varied the development of the municipal system in the two countries. At the precise time when, in northern France, the town

populations were awaking to life, and about to put forth
their energies in the realization of those brilliant historical
episodes which imparted a lustre to the age—the flame of
liberty flashing forth in the darkness of a political night—
the boroughs of England were held in bondage by William
the Conqueror and his barons, fresh from the field of Hastings. Everywhere, the comparative independence they had
enjoyed under Edward the Confessor, had been exchanged
for entire dependence upon the will of the Conqueror, or
of the lords to whom he had transferred possession. While,
then, the French towns were throwing off the yoke of their
feudal masters and attempting to establish republics, the
English burgesses were meditating how much of their
ancient freedom, which had been violently taken from them,
could be regained by purchase from their all-powerful
Norman owners. At Leicester—a town of Roman origin,
subsequently the seat of a Saxon bishopric, and owing to
its central position probably a fair type of contemporary
towns—the first charter procured by the Saxon inhabitants
from their Norman lord, Robert, Earl of Mellent, was dated
in the reign of Henry I., that is, between the years 1100
and 1135 A.D.; when they obtained permission to re-institute
their Merchant Guild, and all the customs they had held
in the reign of the Conqueror, and his son William Rufus.
At the commencement of the twelfth century, therefore,
when some of the French communes had achieved local
independence—had acquired power and importance enough
to make treaties of war and peace with other cities and
potentates—had raised armies and led them to the field under
their own distinctive banners—the towns of England were
plodding on with their local courts and Merchant Guilds,
never dreaming of the acquisition of sovereignty. Thus,
also, while in France many of the cities occupied positions
in the first class, in this country all were in the second and
third class of municipalities.

The rapid, general, and remarkable success of the French communes in the twelfth century could not have been without its influence upon the towns of England, in inspiring their chief inhabitants with a desire to emulate the examples thus set before them; and this was all the more likely as the class of townsmen in this country—those who had commercial intercourse with the people living across the Channel—spoke the French language, which had been introduced by the Norman conquerors, and were accordingly able to hold communication with French citizens. When French merchants visited London and others of our chief places, or English merchants visited the towns of France, they understood each other; so that the story of each successful revolt passed from mouth to mouth, and doubtless as it slowly made its way from population to population aroused the passion for liberty, never dead in this island, and stirred up the townsmen to efforts for their own enfranchisement. It is to this cause, in part at least, we may attribute the fact of king John having granted a larger number of charters to boroughs than were ever granted during the same space of time in any other period of our history.

As remarked of the French communes, so may it be observed of the English boroughs, at this early date,—they sought to secure only "the liberty of going and of coming, of selling and of buying, of being master in one's own house, and of leaving one's property to one's children." They sought, too, freedom from external control, freedom from tolls, and freedom from molestation by the public officers of other districts; and they asked for the rights of pursuing the felons of their own boroughs to the jurisdiction of other communities. In these respects, the local institutions of the two countries resembled each other. The same disposition of town to follow town in the career of municipal progress was witnessed in England which has been recorded of France. Thus, when Henry I. conceded to the citizens of London a charter of privileges, the city of Norwich procured from him a charter embodying the same kind of concessions, and on subsequent occasions the latter manifested the same spirit of imitation and rivalry: and when the burgesses of Newcastle-under-Lyne obtained a charter of privileges from Henry II, the burgesses of Preston procured a similar charter from the same sovereign. Bristol, in the same way, furnished a precedent for Lancaster—Salford for Manchester—and so on in other cases; the text of one charter being closely copied by another, with a few alterations.

The English boroughs seem, however, to have been destined for a longer duration than those of France; and the chief reason may have been in their having assumed a humbler position. The French "communes", it has been seen, set at defiance king and baron, and pushed the issue of the conflict to its extreme limits; avowing their intention to throw off all control, and to exist as republics. The struggle between them and the monarchs of France therefore could not end until either one or other of the belligerent interests had completely subdued the other. Eventually, the kings prevailed. In England, the burgesses were content to make the most advantageous compacts they could with their feudal superiors, and to abide by them; neither desiring nor expecting to overthrow and supplant the local barons and their successors. As both sides acquiesced in the arrangement; as the barons encountered no revolts, and the burgesses experienced no interference in their affairs; the current of events ran, on the whole, smoothly. The previous pages show that exceptions to the rule occurred, as at Norwich and St. Albans; but they do not invalidate the general statement.

But because there were only few battle-pictures presented in the old towns of England, and their stories were, in the main, those of homely progress, it must not be concluded that they played an inconsiderable part in the national history; for, long after most of the French communes had been suppressed by royal proclamation, they were in a state of vigorous existence; ranging themselves on the side of the House of York, indeed, in the great civil war of the fifteenth century. At the decisive battle of Towton, when Edward, duke of York, defeated the forces of the Lancastrian monarch with terrible slaughter, ten at least of the English boroughs—Canterbury, Bristol, Coventry, Salisbury, Worcester, Gloucester, Leicester, Nottingham, Windsor, and Northampton*—contributed by their squadrons, fighting under their town-banners, to obtain so complete a victory for Edward that he was crowned at Westminster three months afterwards. Far more advanced in their views of popular freedom than other boroughs, those of the South saw the advantage to be secured by supporting the Yorkist cause, and therefore assisted its leader to gain the throne of England.

Still, the progress of municipal freedom in the towns of this country was chequered by reverses. Under Henry the Seventh, attempts were made to deprive the mass of the inhabitants of some ancient boroughs of the voice they had hitherto had in the election of the town-councils, and they were excluded from the share they had enjoyed in the administration of local affairs. Instead of being popularly-chosen bodies, the rulers of certain places, constituting local oligarchies, were nominated by the crown, and thereafter left to the appointment of their successors. This was the work of the Tudors; and in the reign of Elizabeth

*See ballad in the library of Trinity College, Dublin, first published by Sir F. Madden, in the *Archaeologia*.

especially it was carried to its consummation. Chiefly owing to the acquisition of property by the local governments of the country, in consequence of the transfer to them, at the Reformation, of the possessions of religious guilds and chantries, to be used for secular public purposes,—a new state of affairs arose, requiring the legal incorporation of the municipal bodies, by virtue of which they could sue and be sued, convey property and hold it, employ a seal, and so forth, under a common name and in a corporate capacity. At the same time, the system of self-election and irresponsible management commenced by Henry the Seventh, was extended and consolidated.

While this *regime* remained in force the Corporations, existing quite independently of the control of the burgesses who were not of their number, had power to elect their Mayors, and other officers, without interference from the crown; but in the reign of Charles the Second and James the Second, even the close Corporations themselves were objects of jealousy to the monarchs. The latter sovereign endeavoured to take away from many of the boroughs their charters, and to fill the local offices with his own nominees; but the result was fatal to his own authority. In attempting, for the promotion of his own purposes, to override the old municipal institutions of the country—narrowed in their operations as they were—the last of the Stuarts took one of the most effectual methods to bring about his own downfall.

The municipalities of the country, modified by the sovereigns of the Tudor dynasty, remained uninterfered with until the Municipal Reform Act (proposed by Lord John Russell) was passed in the year 1835. A commission under the great seal had previously been issued, to inquire into the state of municipal corporations; from whose reports, in 237 places, it was found that the governing body was self-elected in 186 of that number. The institutions which replaced these were founded on the elective principle, and after thirty-two years' experience of their working, they prove to be eminently advantageous to the residents in towns, and satisfactory to the people of England generally. Meanwhile, in France, the great cities and towns yet remain without any power of electing their municipal functionaries: the sovereign appoints the *prefects* and other authorities; and the free communes of the eleventh, twelfth, and thirteenth centuries live only in tradition as the glory of bygone ages.

CHAPTER XVIII.

PRACTICAL CONCLUSIONS.

As the reader will have perceived, the main purpose of this essay has been to trace the origin and describe the development of the municipal institutions of England, by references to local history and ancient documents; to deal with the past and not with the future. But a few observations and suggestions, in reference to the latter, may not be out of place in a work like the present.

For more than thirty years, the leading boroughs of England have been governed by local councils, elected by their inhabitants, which have occupied the place of old corporations, based on a principle of self-election and convicted of gross mal-administration. Meanwhile, the trial of the modern system has been conclusive as to its general success and satisfactory operation. Everywhere, the dwellers in the large towns have experienced the advantages accruing from the management of public property, the regulation of local police, and the adjustment of their various affairs, by responsible representative bodies. There was no novelty in the principles acted upon; for they were simply the ancient constitutional usages revived, as they existed before the accession of the Tudor dynasty. The question hence arises, Is not the extension of the Municipal Reform Act to all communities, capable of self-government, desirable?

Another advance in the direction of self-government has been made, in consequence of the passing of the Health of Towns Act, in the year 1845. Under its provisions, Local Boards have been established in many towns throughout England as yet unprovided with Municipal Councils. In all such localities, the ratepayers have been empowered to levy rates, to execute public works of a certain description, and to exercise control over matters affecting their own civic well-being. They have thus far afforded sufficient evidence of their capacity for managing their own business in these respects. It will be found, on enquiry, that in most of the towns here spoken of, property and charitable institutions exist belonging to the public. The inference is reasonable, that if the Local Boards have proved themselves competent to perform one portion of municipal administration (by no means the least important), they have qualified themselves to fulfil its entire functions. In every town where a Local Board has been in operation, and carried on its proceedings satisfactorily in the main, we may therefore assume that the problem has been solved. In bodies so constituted, the trusteeship of common property might be assuredly vested, and all the authority which legal incorporation confers might be safely placed. The Chairmen of Local Boards might, it may be assumed, appropriately become the Mayors, and the Local Boards themselves the Town Councils, of the boroughs which might be created in the way here suggested.

All that is here proposed is already capable of being effected under the authority of the Municipal Reform Act; but the process required to be gone through is circuitous and costly. It consists in the adoption of a series of measures by the inhabitants of the towns which are favourable to obstructive opposition, and involve an outlay which is often found so formidable as to prove a fatal objection to any scheme of incorporation. What seems to be wanted therefore is a general act constituting Local Boards of Health Corporations, on the same principle as the Municipal Reform Act erected the old Boroughs of England into new boroughs, without calling for the concession of royal charters. The procedure would thus be complete, economical, and universal, in its operation.

It may be objected to the proposal that the towns to be incorporated are too limited in population to justify its acceptance. But when it is remembered that in the early period of our history—as late indeed as the reign of Queen Elizabeth—nearly all the boroughs of this country were inhabited by populations not exceeding 5000 in number, and that in them all the machinery of a municipal administration existed—the objection here stated will disappear. Nor is this all: the modern populations of unincorporated towns possess obvious advantages which the ancient boroughs did not enjoy. Any modern English town includes, for instance, in the ranks of its inhabitants many persons qualified by education and intelligence for taking part in public affairs; while it would have been impossible to have found any person so fitted among the townsmen of the medieval period.

The advantages to be derived from the general enfranchisement of English towns to the extent here suggested would be various. It is not difficult to perceive that the transfer of the feoffments of market-towns from trustees over whom the inhabitants have no control, to their own representatives, would ensure a juster and more satisfactory management of public property than at present. Amenable to the direct influence of their constituents, the administrators of such property would find themselves differently placed from the irresponsible trustees who now have at their sole disposal, in some cases, extensive and valuable estates.

Not merely are social and economical advantages to be regarded in the consideration of this subject. In an age of political activity, political considerations ought also to be entertained. The period in which the idea was possible of retaining men in a condition of pupilage, is passing away; and it is now felt more or less that men are everywhere entitled to the rights of citizenship. To afford, then a channel in which the political energies of townsmen may legitimately flow, is a thing to be desired; and that channel the incorporation of smaller towns, with the accompanying impartation of citizenship, would provide. By offering to the dwellers in every populous community the opportunity of the exercise of a municipal franchise, the state would furnish in truth a "safety valve" for the outlet of the increasing political energy of the people of this country. Not alone would a more impartial administration of local affairs be secured—not alone would a desirable employment of public spirit be presented—by the erection of municipalities in every district of this kingdom; the sense of local interest and self respect of the townsmen, would also find their legitimate gratification in the ability to elect, and the possibility of being elected, managers of their own local affairs. By such means, every district and every inhabitant of it would be elevated to a position in which they would not only become more useful to themselves—they would become, in their joint capacity, so many strong buttresses, supporting the fabric of our constitution.

www.ingramcontent.com/pod-product-compliance
Lightning Source LLC
Chambersburg PA
CBHW020906230426
43666CB00008B/1331